To:

_____

From:

_____

Date:

_____

SHE MADE HERSELF
A HOME

A **PRACTICAL GUIDE** TO DESIGN, ORGANIZE,
AND GIVE PURPOSE TO YOUR SPACE

FEATURING 40+ HOMES

RACHEL VAN KLUYVE

THOMAS NELSON
Since 1798

To my boys and my family. Without you I never would have made it here.

*And to those who pick up this book. It is my hope
that you may have more purpose in your home and,
most importantly, more purpose in your heart.*

Contents

PART 1: GATHERING SPACES

PART 2: RESTFUL PLACES

Introduction

A wise woman builds her home.

—PROVERBS 14:1 NLT

Some of my fondest childhood memories are of helping my mom redecorate our house before my dad got home from work. While he wasn't opposed to redecorating, Dad liked to carefully consider and contemplate each change. But when Mom had a vision for a room, she wanted to bring it to life immediately. She didn't have the patience to wait a minute longer! I remember as soon as Dad's car disappeared from sight, Mom would hurry to clear out a room. She might rearrange furniture, repaint walls, or even paint a furniture piece or two, but she always managed to put the room back together before Dad came home.

When I was old enough to help, she put my hands to good use, teaching me how to bring new life into a space. Then we'd wait with happy anticipation for Dad's reaction as he came through the door.

"Come see what we did!" we'd call, grins stretched across our faces, both thrilled and anxious for him to see the final results.

On more than one occasion, he would say, "I don't see anything different. What am I looking for?"

Mom and I would laugh and tell him all the work we'd finished just minutes before he came through the door. I can still hear Mom's frantic cry, "He's coming down the hill!" as he drove down the driveway.

Oh, the fun I had as a child watching—and later helping—my mom make herself a home. Little did I know, she was passing on her love for homemaking to me.

It's a love that has never left me. When Richard and I first married, I knew I wanted to make our house a home. I wanted it to be something I could be proud of, but I wasn't sure where to start, so I just copied the trends and designs of the time. When I look back at some of the design choices I made, I'm horrified! But I'm still proud of the love and effort I poured into those early attempts at creating my home. After changing wall colors many times, removing and re-laying flooring, and painting the kitchen with my own two hands, I began to develop my own sense of style, and that inspired me to keep going.

My husband and I have been designing in some capacity for well over a decade now, from real estate design to our own custom-built home. With each project, our style and taste have evolved. When I started my blog called *Crate and Cottage* in January 2017, I wanted to share my passion for design. I blogged about my DIYs, Goodwill finds, and the journey of building our home, hoping I could encourage other women and teach them a few design tricks along the way. Seeing my work featured in some of my favorite places—from social media and blogs to bigger names like *The Farmhouse Movement* magazine, Wayfair, Pier 1, *Better Homes & Gardens*, and *Style Me Pretty Living*—has given me confidence in my design skills and fueled my passion for what I share. The whole journey has been a blessing, but the most unexpected and meaningful part has been finding a community of women who also want to learn how to create a home they can be proud of, a place with *purpose*.

This book includes the most important things I've learned in my years of designing homes. You'll also get great design tips from some of my favorite women who create beautiful, organized homes. They may not hold degrees in design, and most won't even claim to be an expert in the field, but they have captured my heart with their talent and their desire to make a home with purpose. The photos you see across these pages aren't stock images or artificial spaces set up just for this book. These are photos of my real-life, lived-in home and the homes of women from my online community.

My hope is that these pages spark your passions, guide you to create spaces you love, and most importantly, give you the confidence to try something new. Anyone—no matter her age, status, income level, or past—can make a home for herself and those she loves. Friends, as you look at the beautiful homes featured throughout this book, remember this lesson I first learned from my mom: if she made herself a home, so can you!

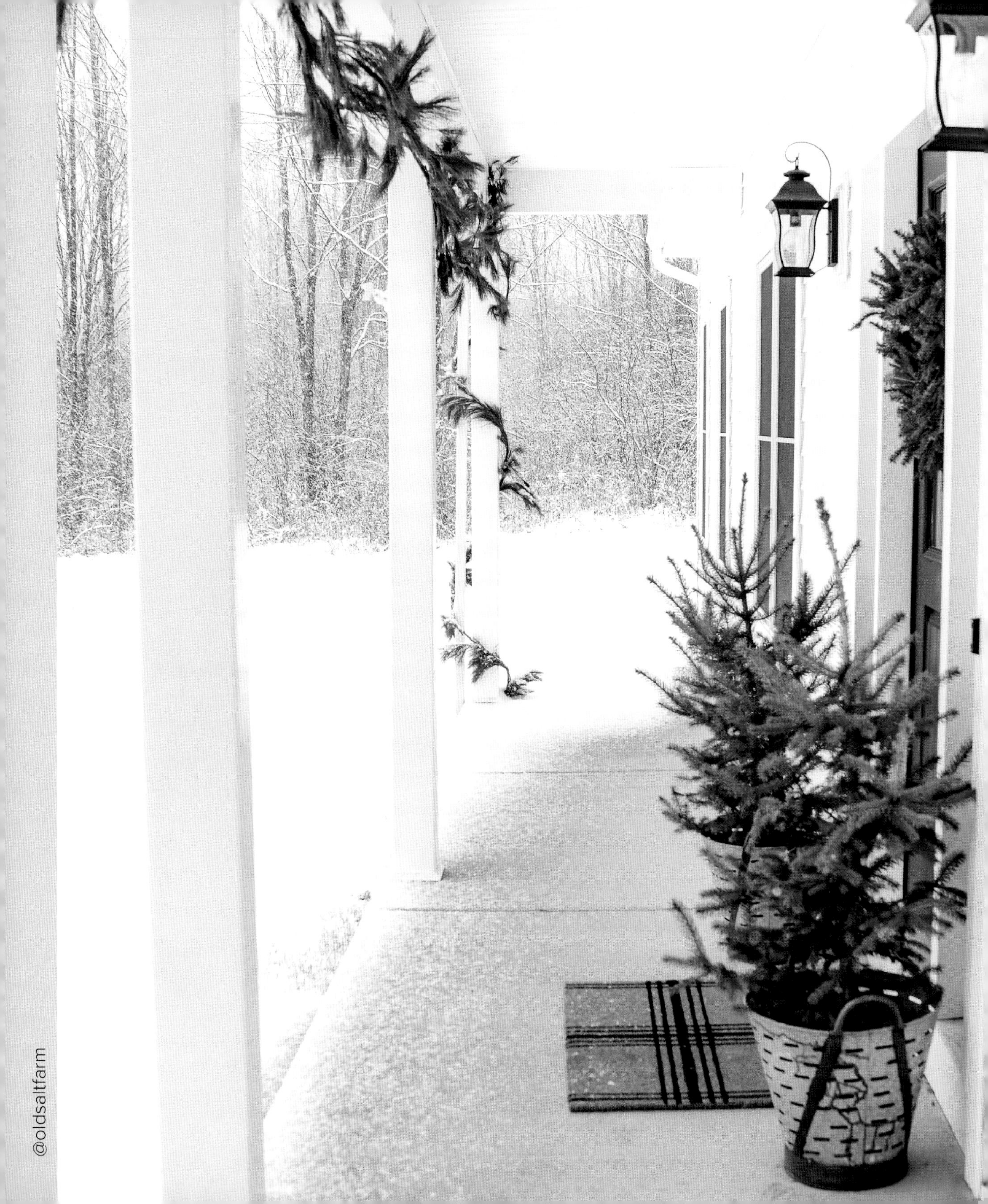

@oldsaltfarm

Find Your Why

The best journey takes you home.

Have you ever thought about what makes a house a home? A *house* is simply a structure made for living, but a *home* provides a sense of refuge, security, and love. That comforting feeling doesn't happen by accident—it's created when your space has a specific purpose and fits a plan for how you want to live.

When we started building our house in January of 2017, I realized I wanted to create a space filled with a feeling of togetherness. So I prayed for our doors to always be open and for our home to offer a sense of peace and welcome to all who entered. I'm an introvert, so this prayer wasn't always easy; it often pushed me out of my comfort zone. But it became what I call my *why*, my *purpose*.

I used all I had learned about design and organization to make my space feel open, warm, and inviting, a place where people are loved and accepted, where grace is freely given. Then, because I had designed our home with that purpose in mind, it became much easier to open the doors, host the parties, gather the neighborhood kids for a swim, or invite the new neighbors over for dinner. My home intentionally fulfills my *why*.

What is your *why*? What kind of home do you want to create? What purpose do you want it to serve? Before you look at a paint chip or move a chair, I encourage you to sit down with pen and paper and thoughtfully define your *why*—the purpose of your home. These questions will get you started:

- Do you want to create a sense of togetherness in a world that is so busy?
- Do you want to share your love of cooking with others?
- Do you want a place where your whole family can comfortably visit?
- Do you want to create a place that is peaceful, a refuge for your busy life?

Finding your *why* will help you define how you want your space to function and allow you to more easily navigate through your style and design decisions.

WORDS TO LIVE BY

Once you have your *why*, choose a motto to guide you in living it out, like a cherished verse, a favorite quote, or your own carefully crafted words to live by. My family's motto is a Bible verse from Psalm 25:4–5 (NLT), and we plastered it right on our wall:

> Show me the right path, O LORD;
>   point out the road for me to follow.

@simplysoutherncottage

> Lead me by your truth and teach me,
>   for you are the God who saves me.
>   All day long I put my hope in you.

That verse captures our family's beliefs and mission: to follow God, to do His will, and to do it together. And I believe at least part of His will for my family is to make others feel welcome, needed, and served—both in our home and in our lives. As we try to be His hands and feet in a tangible way, seeing these words each day is a visual reminder of the kind of life we want to live and the kind of home we want to create. Your motto should do the same. It should remind you of your *why* and inspire you to live it.

GETTING STARTED

Armed with your *why* and your motto, you have a clear guide to lead you as you make design decisions. And believe it or not, you'll find yourself coming back to these two things and remembering, *This is what I want. This is why I am thankful. This is what I am working to create.* As Sally Clarkson wrote, "One cannot build what has not been imagined. And one cannot bring a vision to life without a plan." Create your plan first, then create your design.

To begin creating that plan, walk through the rooms and halls of your home and dream about how to execute your *why*. What would make your space more relaxing? A little more organized and efficient? Think about what energizes and equips you, what inspires you and gives you room to grow.

Remember that creating a home is a process. It doesn't happen overnight. It's going to involve rolling up your sleeves and getting to work. You have to toss Pinterest perfection out the window (although it can be helpful for ideas and inspiration). Ideally, you'll do some shopping with family and friends, and then we'll dive in together—one shelf, one corner, one lovely room at a time, all the while finding purpose and joy along the way.

Choosing to create a home built around your *why* and the people you love is the beginning, the first step. The rest will follow.

Let's go home, shall we?

@featherglass

Styles and Colors

Let love color your home.

STYLES

Once you have your purpose in mind, it's time to think about your style. What makes a room beautiful and comfortable to you? We usually know what appeals to us even if we can't pinpoint a reason why. We're drawn to certain colors, furniture pieces, and décor items but may not know how to pull all those colors and pieces together to create a cohesive style that reflects who we are.

In many ways, choosing your style can be the most intimidating and stressful part of the design process, but it doesn't have to be! First, take the style quiz on page xx to find your favorite design style. I chose a rustic style, and

because I like my rooms to have a cohesive look, I've used that style throughout the house by sticking with a neutral color palette and placing antiques here and there. I would suggest using a cohesive style for your home too. Once you've chosen your favorite style, it's then easy to build on that look in each room. While there are many variations of styles, I have chosen to break them down into four main groups: rustic, traditional, modern, and eclectic.

Rustic Style

A rustic style incorporates a flea market kind of shopping, using thrifted or antique finds along with newer pieces often made to look old. Within rustic style you will see raw, natural woods and a neutral color palette revolving around shades of taupe, white, and gray. People often use antique items to achieve a more rustic look, or they may try to recreate that chipped and vintage feel by distressing newer items.

The well-known farmhouse style is a subcategory of rustic that pulls in galvanized metal, raw wood, and farmlike finds. There is also a rustic version of what some call "shabby chic." This style is brought to life by furniture items that show great wear and tear. In general, the rustic style seeks to combine the aesthetics of vintage finds and rustic, natural surroundings.

Traditional Style

A traditional style is one that focuses on the timeless and classic with nothing too wild or out of the ordinary. It is more of an evolution of European décor, mixing styles from various centuries of design. The colors are subtle but warm in tone. Traditional homes feel both comfortable and elegant. The traditional-style home emphasizes uniformity and symmetry with carefully placed, matching items such as chairs, lamps, artwork, and tables. Furniture is often upholstered in muted or patterned fabrics, wood tones are dark and rich, and window coverings that feature classic lines are a must. Subcategories of the traditional style include coastal and colonial.

A coastal style creates the relaxed ease of beach life. It's defined by shades of oceanlike blue, white, and neutral colors. Soft textures beckon you to unwind and relax. Sea grasses, shells, glass, and other natural textures find their way into the coastal-style home.

The colonial style, like coastal, is known for its subtle, subdued colors with an emphasis on wood and natural elements. There is much attention to detail. Wainscoting, patterned wallpaper, and polished floors and furniture are hallmarks of this style. The colonial style, while still elegant, focuses more on handcrafted elements.

Modern Style

Despite its name, the modern style isn't new; rather, it stems from an early twentieth-century Scandinavian design. Its focus is on simple, clean lines and earth-toned, neutral color palettes. Modern style emphasizes form and shape with a very distinctive architecture. You won't find a lot of fluff or pattern in the modern style. Instead, it uses natural elements like leather, wood, and metal. It features straighter lines and utilizes steel, chrome, and glass.

In recent years, the modern farmhouse style has become popular. A modern farmhouse steers away from the country vintage feel of the more rustic farmhouse. Instead, it integrates the coziness and textures of a farmhouse design with accents of modern linear furniture and furnishings. Other popular subcategories of the modern style are the industrial and minimalist styles. If you eliminate clutter and focus on simplicity, you can create a minimalist home under any style category, but much of minimalist design leans toward the modern style. Industrial is a newer rendition of modern and can also be tailored to other style categories. An industrial modern style is achieved by using metal and wood tones, with more modern furnishings. Exposed rafters, duct work, and piping are hallmarks of the industrial modern style.

Eclectic Style

An eclectic style is a more universal style with elements from all eras, all color families, and all design styles available to use. If you enjoy items from a variety of design categories and centuries, and if you aren't worried about matching items or symmetry or subtle color blending, then the eclectic style might be for you. The eclectic style isn't an excuse to just throw anything into a room, but it does allow you to deliberately mix in the items you love, regardless of their individual style. Subcategories of the eclectic style include bohemian and vintage.

Bohemian style focuses on color and culture. Textures take on many shapes and forms, not only in the textiles but also on the walls. To have a boho-style home means you love a more relaxed and nontraditional way of decorating. Natural plant elements, bright patterned rugs, woven baskets, and rich leathers and textiles are all elements of a bohemian home.

The vintage-style home can also be considered eclectic, pulling in pieces from different eras. For example, while the farmhouse is my primary style with its rustic pieces and chippy, shabby chic furniture, I also have some elements of the vintage style in my own home, giving it a bit of an eclectic air. I love to add vintage pieces from different eras, such as the 1890s hutch in my dining area and my grandmother's early 1900s wash stand, which I converted into a vanity for our half bath. A vintage home reflects a love of history and a desire to remember the past.

COLORS

After you've chosen a basic style, make it personal by picking a color scheme. Do you prefer a neutral palette of whites, beiges, and grays? Or do you love complementary colors, leaning more toward yellows and purples, oranges and blues, or greens and reds? If your home already has a neutral base, I suggest bringing color in through accessories so that the eye is drawn to the objects filling the space. If you love a darker wall or brighter palette, try keeping your furniture and décor light and neutral.

For inspiration, check out the displays of your favorite shops, scroll through photos on social media, and flip through home décor books (like this one!) to help you discover your likes and dislikes. Find several photos of rooms you like and study them.

- What draws you to those rooms?
- Do they have a common color scheme?
- Is there one color that always catches your eye?

You can also find color inspiration in the world around you—in outfits, paintings, nature, or anything else!

Finding your color scheme is a big part of defining your style. Keep in mind that certain colors complement certain styles. For example, a rustic style tends to use white and wood tones. A traditional style focuses on rich patterns and a more subtle color palette of taupes and light grays, while a modern style leans more toward a nature-inspired color palette. Because the eclectic style often features a mix of patterns and colors in its furnishings, the color palette for walls and floors is usually more neutral.

Though color and style tend to go hand in hand, don't be afraid to experiment and mix it up a little. Take time to figure out which colors fill you with a sense of joy and peace. When you incorporate those colors into your design, you'll find yourself smiling every time you walk through your home.

START

Where do you prefer to shop for décor?

| Trendy department stores. | *– or –* | Antique malls, flea markets, and secondhand stores. |

Which dining room do you love?

What do you prefer on your walls?

| Not a lot. I like simplicity. | *– or –* | Fill 'er up! I like to display all my favorite things. |

What's your favorite bedroom aesthetic?

| Classic chandelier with soft, light bedding. | *– or –* | Shiplap and galvanized materials. |

MODERN   **TRADITIONAL**

...at's your go-to color palette?

Neutrals, please! *– or –* I love color!

What wall treatment can you not live without?

| Wainscoting and board-and-batten. | *– or –* | Funky wallpaper. |

...ixed pieces, ...ilts, macramé, ...d bold colors.

...STIC

ECLECTIC

Gathering Spaces

Home is where your story begins.

Our home is open to others most evenings. And while it's nice to have my family alone a few nights a week, it's equally nice to have friends and family come through our doors on a regular basis. No matter the time or day, my kids often ask, "Who is coming over?" It warms my heart to know they expect our doors to always be open.

"What day is it, Mom?" my nine-year-old asks.

"Friday."

"Does that mean someone's coming over?"

Even my three-year-old asks, "Who's next, Mama?"

And that's just how I want it to be.

Gathering is our passion, though more so for my extroverted husband. But I've learned to embrace the good and the bad of hosting. It's a way of pushing myself to reach out to others, to show love to our family and our community. To gather is to come together, to be welcomed into a space. This can be as simple as a family movie night or coffee with friends, and it can be as elaborate as hosting a baby shower or dinner party. Either way, gathering requires a gathering space.

Gathering spaces are those places in the home where you want people to, well, gather. They're also the places people naturally tend to wander

To gather is to come together, to be welcomed into a space.

into and linger. Whether it's a party in the living room, a family dinner in the kitchen, a card game spread across the coffee table, or a fireside spot to watch the game, these are the spaces that bring people together. As you begin to think of creating your own gathering spaces, consider your *why*. What purpose do you want these spaces to serve?

- Do you want to entertain? Or are you looking to create a quiet area where you can gather with loved ones to be refreshed and renewed after a long day?
- Do you want a space for cozy conversations with close friends? Or room for large parties where the whole neighborhood is welcome?
- Do you want to create a place where games are played and laughter is shared?
- Do you want a space where all of your fellow sports fans can gather on couches and cheer on the team in front of the TV?

Once you've determined the kind of gatherings you want in your home, it's time to ask yourself these two questions:

1. **Where do you want these gathering spaces to be?**
   - What spaces in your home are best suited for the gatherings you envision? The living room, bonus room, or kitchen and dining area?
   - Do these spaces already exist? Are you already using them for gathering purposes?
   - Is your home equipped for larger gatherings? Or is it better suited to serve just your immediate family?
2. **How can the layout and furnishings of these spaces serve you and your family, as well as those you want to welcome in?**
   - Do you need more seating for the family and friends you want to gather?
   - Do you need more tables for holding games, books, or food and drinks?

@angelarose_diyhome

@beautifulchaos.home

- Do you need to change the layout so there is more open space?

As you answer these questions, remember your *why*, your purpose. Write it on a notecard, a pretty piece of stationery, or even a paint chip. Put it wherever you'll see it as you make your design decisions. Because, yes, thinking about the physical room and layout is important, but even more important is making sure that the space you create does what you want it to do. Keep your purpose at the forefront of your decisions. It will help launch you into the design and enable you to shop for those pieces that will make your gathering spaces more practical. And as we walk through my home and through the designs of some amazingly talented women, take your *why* with you. It might help you take the ideas you get from these pages and transform them into practical ways to enhance your home.

Come on in. Let's gather.

Show me the right
path, O Lord; point
out the road for me to
follow. Lead me by your
truth and teach me,
for you are the God who
saves me. All day long
I put my hope in you.

Psalms 25: 4-5

Chapter 1

ENTRYWAY

Home is where the heart is.

The entryway is your first and last place of gathering. It's your welcoming hello and your well-wished good-bye. Whether you have a tiny apartment foyer, a small stoop, a lavish wraparound porch, or simply a door, the old adage is true: first impressions are the most lasting. And the entryway is your guests' first hint of what to expect once they're inside. In our business of showing and listing homes, it's always the well-kept doorways, porches, and entryways that buyers respond to immediately. That's because the care taken on the outside is usually a reflection of what's inside.

The entryway is your first and last place of gathering. It's your welcoming hello and your well-wished good-bye.

Just as the entryway is important for welcoming guests, so is the greeting itself. When I was a kid, my mom and dad always greeted our guests at the door. From taking our guests' coats and bags to lighting our home with candles, my parents made sure our guests knew they were happy to have them. It's something I do now for our guests. In fact, my entire family likes to greet our guests at the door. The kids hug friends, and we are there to take coats or bags and to help with any need they might have. From the design of our entryway to the warmth of our smiles, my family and I strive to create an atmosphere of welcome.

So what does an entryway look like, you ask? Well, let's step inside and talk layout.

LAYOUT AND STYLE

If you're thinking the design of your home doesn't allow you to have an actual entryway, don't be discouraged. You would be surprised by what a few simple changes can do to define a space. For example, a small side table tucked against the wall with a mirror above and hooks nearby for coats says, *Hello and welcome! Put your things down here and come inside.*

In my own home I have a six-foot-long wall. I simply placed a narrow console table along that wall and then added a few of my favorite décor items, a welcoming rug, and a fun chandelier. A mirror hangs over the table to make the space feel larger.

Many homes have a coat closet. Take a look at how @theschmidthome used hers to create a welcoming entryway. By removing the clothing rod and building a bench for seating, her family and guests now have a place to sit and slip shoes on or off. Baskets provide a place for gadgets and personal items, hooks are ready to hold coats and purses, and a shelf underneath the bench holds shoes. Because

@theschmidthome

The door itself is as much a part of your guests' experience as actually walking in. Create a welcoming scene that makes your guests smile and want to step inside. Hang a seasonal wreath or sign. Lay out a welcome mat. Adorn your stoop with pumpkins, small potted trees, or florals for the season. Not only is this a happy welcome for your guests, but it's a happy welcome for you and your family to enjoy each time you walk through the door.

Step Inside

Now step through the door and into your home. Remember your *why* and your family's motto.

- Is this space fulfilling the purpose you've set for your home?
- What do you want your guests to see first?
- Is there a place for coats, purses, or umbrellas on rainy days?
- Is there enough room for a table, a mirror, or some art?

Peruse your favorite magazines and home décor blogs to find more inspiration. A thoughtfully designed entryway is a simple and welcoming way to take care of your guests from the moment they walk in your home.

the design makes the purpose of this space clear, guests know exactly what to do with their things. Use the examples in this chapter to help you start visualizing your own space. Here are a few more tips on layout.

Start at the Door

Step outside your home and imagine being a guest walking up to knock on the door. Does your porch—or stoop or door— feel welcoming?

@featherglass

Making It Work

Once you've evaluated your space, it's time to start thinking about what you need to make it work. Here are some of my favorite tips to get you started.

Shop your own home first. Using something you already have is a great way to make something old feel new again. Perhaps it's a piece that's underutilized in another room.

- Would that small table from the bedroom work better in the entryway?
- Could that unused chair be tucked into a corner to hold bags or coats?
- How about gathering some wall prints from around the home to create a gallery wall?

KEEP IT *Tidy*

Keeping your porch or stoop clean and clutter-free is a great way to welcome guests (and yourself) to your home. Sweep the porch often to clear away debris and unwanted bugs. Pluck dead leaves from plants, and replace your welcome mat when it has become worn from welcoming family and friends. Changing out seasonal décor is also a fun way to mix it up and make your entry feel fresh and new.

Create a drop zone. Whether your entryway is just for you or for guests, everyone needs a place to drop his or her belongings. Some homes have more than one entry, but if this is your only entrance, make it functional for you. That can be as simple as a small side table with a bowl or basket for phones and keys.

Little touches matter. Is a rug all you have space for? Well then, do just that. Simply adding a rug can help define the space as an entry. If possible, hang a mirror to bring in light and help the space feel more open. Think of small ways to make a grand gesture. A vase with flowers—real or faux—always cheers up a space. And a basket or two tucked underneath the entry table provides much-needed storage.

Try something bold. If you have the space—and the time and money, of course—you can be bolder with your design. Paint the walls. Add some texture with wallpaper, shiplap, or board-and-batten. Deconstruct a hall closet and turn it into the space you need. If you need help, check out some DIY videos on YouTube. They can turn even daunting projects into a simple step-by-step process. Don't be afraid to be bold.

Venture out. When you've done all you can with what you have, *then* it's time to venture out to the stores. Shopping is my favorite part of design, but it usually comes at the very end. Scour your favorite local shops as well as online retailers. And don't forget to check out local antique and consignment stores, garage sales, and estate sales. Find items that flow naturally with the rest of your home. Do you love color and bright vibes? Look for pieces that pop. If you prefer a more neutral and natural feel, go with soft tones, wooden mirrors, and shades of white. Make your entryway a place that welcomes you as well as your guests.

Your entryway sets the tone for the rest of your home, so make your guests feel welcome with a thoughtfully arranged layout and a place to stash their things. Greet your guests at the door with a smile, and let them know they are valued and accepted. Then let the gathering begin!

@beesnburlap

Our foyer was like any other foyer until the 5 came along. One day I decided to draw and paint the 5 on the door for the five members of our family, and it has been a hit ever since! My family loves it, and so does everyone else who sees it. I love industrial vintage pieces, so this area has a bit of both. Between the black brick wallpaper, white and black décor, and the vintage mantel, our foyer is anything but typical now!

@plankandpillow

We wanted to create a modern farmhouse feel as soon as you walk in our front door. We did this by using painted knotty pine shiplap on the walls of our foyer and industrial black metal railing on our stairs. It creates a nice contrast of rustic and modern.

@thegingerhome

Nothing says home like a front porch swing! Adding a porch swing to the front of our house made it feel instantly welcoming, and the swing invites family and friends to sit and chat.

Don't forget curb appeal. Accessorizing your outdoor spaces can add charm to your home. Pillows, throws, lanterns, planters, a pretty doormat— it's the details that make your house feel warm and inviting!

@themorrismanor

Adding a large mirror and functional storage to the foyer keeps the space feeling open and airy.

Style ON A BUDGET

Well-lit entries make coming home more welcoming for you and easier to navigate for your guests. Online stores have some of the greatest deals on lighting, and they have so many options, from flush-mount fixtures and chandeliers to exterior lights.

Amazon was a lifesaver for me during our build. Take this barn light, for example. We used it on both our front and back porches, and it was less than $35. And best of all? They deliver it right to your door!

WHERE TO SHOP

ENTRY TABLES
- Walmart
- Wayfair

MIRRORS
- Goodwill
- Hobby Lobby
- Target
- T.J.Maxx

BASKETS
- Hobby Lobby
- Pier 1
- T.J.Maxx

LAMPS
- At Home Store
- Target
- T.J.Maxx
- Walmart

RUGS
- Amazon
- eSaleRugs.com
- Pier 1
- RugsUSA.com
- Target
- T.J.Maxx
- Wayfair

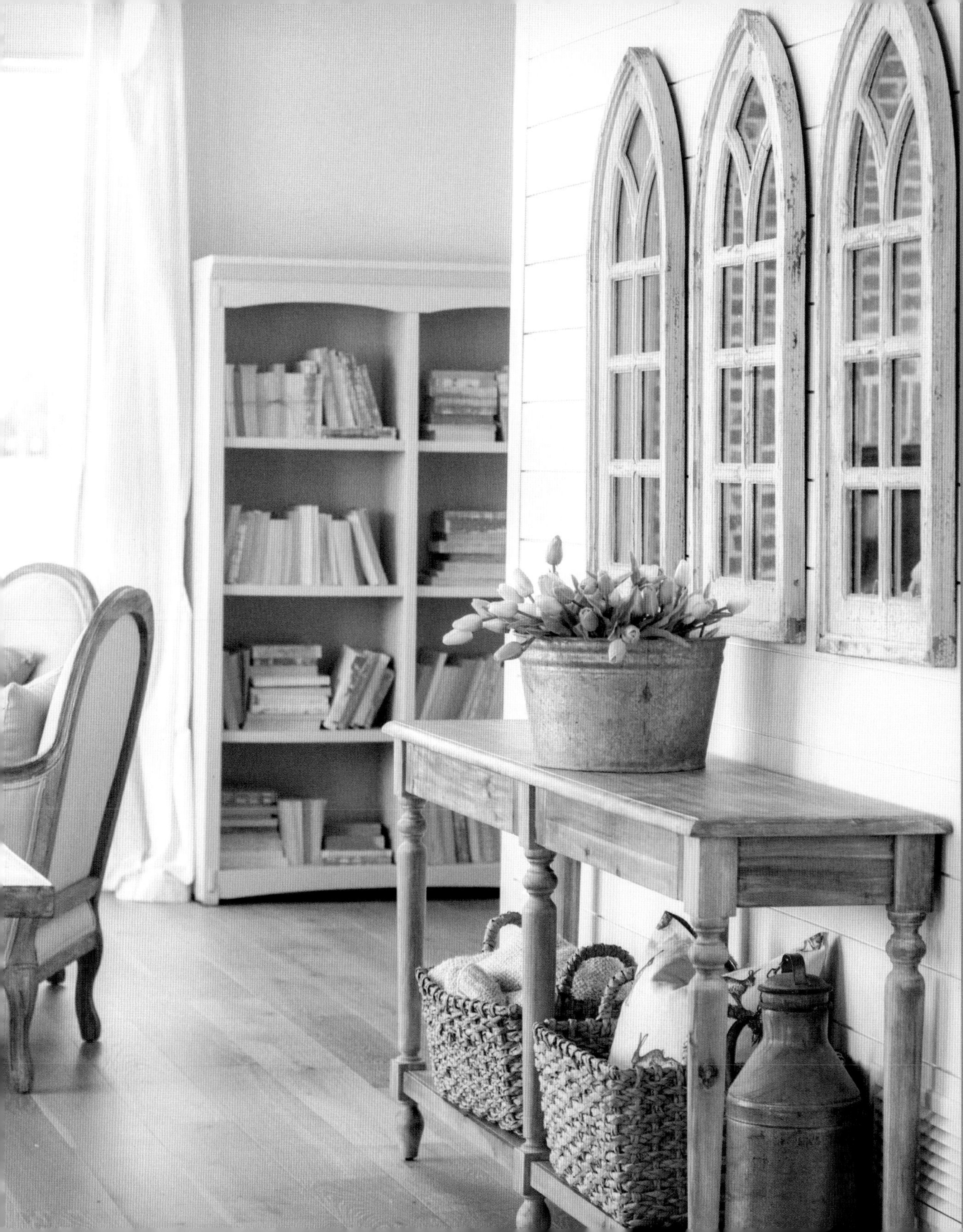

@handmade.farmhouse

MAKE YOUR HOUSE A *Home*

RACHEL VAN KLUYVE
www.CrateandCottage.com
@crateandcottage

When people ask me why I want to share this book with so many amazing women, I tell them my story. I started my social media platform for three reasons: to have something for myself that uses my talents, to meet wonderful people, and to do something for the greater good.

During the first six months of joining Instagram, I reached out to several influencers for advice on growing a platform. One of my first real connections was a phone call I had with Alicia Armstrong @ourvintagenest—and the thought of that conversation still touches my heart today. Alicia explained the process of creating an online community, guided me, and gave me advice. She didn't know me; she helped me out of the goodness of her heart. Because of her willingness to help "the little guy," I began to develop a relationship with her and many others.

A year into my journey, I felt the Lord whisper, "Let's use this social media for good." A few weeks later I reached out to a nonprofit that builds schools for girls in a least-developed country. The stories about the girls' needs touched my heart, and I put together a group of ten large Instagram influencers. We each shared the story of these beautiful girls, and by the end of the fundraiser, we had raised enough money from generous individuals

across the world to put twenty-eight girls into school for a year. I remember crying when it was over. Just a small connection with these women, each using their platforms to spread awareness, changed the lives of girls thousands of miles away. It still reminds me of the beauty and good that can come from social media.

After that event I continued to grow my online community. We regularly build each other up with encouragement and advice. It's taught me that community is everything, support is necessary, and giving back is crucial. This is why I have such a deep desire to feature other women in this book. I've asked a few of them to share who they are and how they've made their houses into homes, including their mottoes for life, their *whys*, their favorite tips, and photos of their beautiful homes. It's my hope that seeing each photo and hearing each story shared in this book will give you that same sense of community I have and also give you confidence that you too can make a difference while you make your house a home.

FIVE MUST-HAVES

1 A WREATH AND A WELCOME MAT

These simple touches instantly warm up an entryway and say, "Welcome!" They give a glimpse into the heart of your home, plus they're a fun way to be creative and are easily changed for the seasons.

Not sure which wreath is right for you? Take a drive around town and check out the entryways of local florists and boutiques—they'll often inspire you with their creations. Dare to think outside the box: I bought embroidery hoops for $5 at Hobby Lobby. By simply adding some faux green garland, I created simple, classic wreaths for my front doors in less than fifteen minutes (see page 4).

2 A RUG

A rug will designate even the smallest of spaces as the entryway. Look for a rug that not only reflects your design style but also holds up to the weather and traffic. Jute is always a great option. It works with most any style and can stand the test of comings and goings.

3 DROP ZONE, DROP ZONE!

When there isn't a designated drop zone, keys, phones, shoes, coats, and all those other essentials seem to get scattered all over the house. Guests can end up carrying keys and bags with them when they aren't sure what to do with their things. Create a practical area where stuff can be dropped. This may mean adding hooks, buying a small console table, or even breaking down a coat closet. But whatever it looks like for your home, create a space to drop your things.

4 ART AND A MIRROR

Much like a rug, art creates what I like to call a small *scene*, and it can serve to designate the space as its own area. If you have room, hang a piece of art that speaks to you and makes you smile. If you can, add a mirror to bring in light and the illusion of space.

5 LIGHTING

Switch out your builder-grade, flush-mount lighting for something fun. YouTube is a great resource for learning how to change out lighting. If DIY isn't for you, a local handyman can do it quickly and inexpensively. In my own entryway I used a neutral beaded chandelier to match my farmhouse style and to set the tone for the rest of the house.

@pineandprospecthome

Chapter 2

LIVING ROOM

There's no place like home.

O nce you've welcomed your guests through the entryway, it's time to entertain them—and what better place to do that than in your central gathering space? The living room is where you can relax and have good conversations—and have fun! It's where you sit with your best friend and share your heart over a cup of coffee, where you curl up with a magazine after a long day's work, and where you sprawl on the floor for Saturday morning games with your kids. People spend most of their together time in the living room, and I don't know of any house, apartment, or mansion that doesn't have some designated area for this gathering space.

The living room is where good conversations take place, relaxation occurs, and fun is had.

Intentionality here is important. My dear friend and mentor Deb is everything I want to be when I grow up. She is my hero, and it's because of her welcoming heart. Her joy and love for others shines through in everything she does, from how she cooks and entertains to how she lives her life serving others. Each time I visit her home, she greets me with a smile and hug—and sometimes even a hand-lettered note on her chalkboard sign! She whisks away my coat and bag, all the while complimenting my outfit. Then she pulls me into her living room and serves tea on a beautiful tray, usually accompanied by some sweet treat she has prepared herself. From the minute I arrive to the moment I leave, Deb is thinking of me. She exudes warmth and hospitality, and this is the feeling I want to carry into my space.

Spreading joy is a part of my purpose, my *why*, for our living room, so I have intentionally created a space that encourages just that. Ask yourself what you want out of the spaces you invite people into and what you can do to create it.

Come and sit, and let's talk living rooms.

LAYOUT AND STYLE

A living room should be for just that: *living*. Ask yourself what you want out of your space. Is it the family-gathering space, the laughing-with-friends space, or the asking-your-husband-about-his-day-because-you-rarely-get-a-moment-alone space? What would you like to intentionally use this space for?

After you've thought about the type of living you want to do, make your plan. Not the plan for a perfectly curated, look-but-don't-touch space—the plan for intentionally living with the people you love.

For me, it's easy to get so caught up in my to-do list that I miss out on my to-live list. Just the other day, one of my kiddos asked if he could to go to Grandma's so he would have someone to play with him. Those, my friend, are moments of clarity. I abandoned my sink full of dirty dishes, asked him what he'd like to play, then sprawled out on our living room floor to enjoy some time together. Who cares about the dishes anyway, right?

I know we all have full plates and long lists, and I'm not advocating that we stop taking care of our homes, but every single day I'm learning more about how to prioritize

my tasks and lists and add more life-giving moments like these:

- Family game night
- Friday movies, complete with popcorn or a favorite snack
- Date-night-in with my husband
- Dinner with friends

Whatever you choose as the purpose of your living room, make sure the layout fits that purpose. For example, when we built our home, the living room was very important to us. I had prayed my introverted heart would be open to entertaining and I would make all those who entered our doors feel welcome.

That desire played a major role in my design. Since I wanted our living room to exude a feeling of togetherness, one of our first decisions was to have all our interior rooms branch off from the large living space. We also set up the space to invite conversation—with our couches facing each other, not a TV. In fact, we don't have a TV anywhere downstairs. An open-concept design allows our living room, dining room, and kitchen to work together as one large space. (I don't want to miss out on part of the party because I'm off cleaning the kitchen!) I realize not all homeowners have the option of an open concept or a custom build, but no matter the size

or shape of your living room, you *can* create a space that fits your purpose.

So what purpose do you want your living room to serve?

- Does your family love watching sports? Focus the room around the TV.
- Do you play games and need a table area? Incorporate a side table or coffee table for your family or guests to sit around.
- Do you love to relax and prop up your feet? Do you like daily power naps in your recliner? Make room for chairs that offer plenty of room for stretching out, or use ottomans that are perfect for resting tired feet.

Take a moment to write down all the ways you want to use your living room, then rank them. These notes will help you design your space in a way that perfectly fits your family's needs.

Remember, the layout of your space is where purpose and functionality meet. Start by measuring the space, and if you're a visual person, map it out on paper. Note the dimensions of your existing pieces and add those to your drawing. Play around with the layout, rearranging what you already have. Then evaluate your needs.

- Do you need more or less seating?
- Can you comfortably fit a large sectional, or do you need a smaller daybed sofa?
- What are the best table and shelving options for your space and needs?
- Which pieces do you want or need to add?
- What dimensions should the new pieces be?

KEEP IT *Tidy*

If your living room is, well, *lived in*, you probably have items that need to be contained. Clutter creates visual stress. Make your space more peaceful and inviting by clearing away toys, blankets, and magazines when you aren't using them. My motto is if everything has a home, clutter won't exist. For example, because my kids know where their toys live, they are more likely to put them away. (And I'm more likely to return my own clutter to its home too!)

I use a few tricks to keep the mess hidden while allowing my space to be functional: baskets, clear totes hidden under couches or in hall closets, and ottomans full of toys are my go-tos. If magazines are your thing, hide them in a large basket by the couch. If you're obsessed with blankets, consider a coffee table that opens up for storage. There are so many storage options—find what works for you.

The layout of your space is where purpose and functionality meet.

Now, let's think about style. Do the pieces you have reflect the style you've chosen? If you've figured out which style you love, and nothing you own reflects that style, make a change. If you want a more modern look, your grandmother's antique chair and side table probably won't fit. Consider updating your pieces by painting them a darker or lighter color, reupholstering fabrics, or changing out knobs. If that isn't an option, or if what you update still doesn't feel like "you," consider getting something that better suits your style. I know it's hard to part with or change sentimental items. Remind yourself that Grandma (or whoever passed down furniture to you) would have wanted that piece to bring you joy,

and the fact that you're reusing it is beautiful in itself.

Evaluate: Does It Work?

Once you've found the pieces you love and placed them in your space, take some time to evaluate the layout. Move them around and see which layout works best.

For me, I have to physically see my plan laid out before I know if it works. I test the couch along one wall and then along another one. I shift the rug and move the side tables around until they fit the room's functionality.

And don't worry if it doesn't work out right away. I can't tell you how many times I have rearranged rooms only to realize I liked it better the way it was before. I have also laid out a space one way and then realized a week later it wasn't going to work. Sometimes you need to live in the space for a while. Take the time to make sure its purpose is being fulfilled. Is it functioning the way you envisioned it? If not, what changes can you make?

Designing a home to actually live in—as opposed to one set up for a photo shoot—takes time. Chances are, you'll need to make some adjustments, and that's okay. Relax and enjoy this process of making yourself a home.

Style ON A BUDGET

There is no need to break the bank on furniture and home décor. I once furnished an entire model home with three bedrooms, a living room, and kitchen for $5,000. How, you ask? Deals! After searching for barely used items on Facebook Marketplace and OfferUp, I head to retailers like IKEA, T.J.Maxx, Marshalls, and Hobby Lobby for small décor items.

And just a tip: don't spend a lot of money on table lamps. I have already replaced mine twice because, well, I have boys. Personally, I don't like to invest a lot in accessories. I want my house to be livable. If something breaks, I'm not worried, because I didn't spend a fortune on it.

WHERE TO SHOP

COUCHES
- Ashley Furniture HomeStore
- Home Depot's Home Decorators Collection
- IKEA, especially their slipcovered sofas
- Macy's

LIGHTING
- Hobby Lobby
- T.J.Maxx
- Walmart's Better Homes & Gardens line

PILLOW COVERS
- Amazon
- Hobby Lobby

TABLES
- Facebook Marketplace
- Goodwill
- OfferUp
- Pier 1

@beautifulchaos.home

@keely.mann

You can easily pull off an authentic farmhouse look by blending old with new. Order that brand-new slipcovered sofa, but add in found pieces to give the room a seasoned character. For example, use accent tables made of salvaged wood and add old architectural pieces on mantels and walls.

Don't be afraid to go bold with color.

@onelittlemomma

One of my favorite ways to add texture, dimension, and interest to a space is with rugs. I love big rugs, and my favorite thing is to double up those rugs. I've even triple-layered rugs before! Try using natural texture rugs under a patterned or a thick high-pile rug. If your rug is small, add a bigger raffia or natural-fiber rug underneath it. It will fill the space and add depth to the room!

@thetailoredhaven

Want to create the coziest space? Drape a throw over a sofa or chair, and create a puddle on the floor. Even the kitty agrees!

MAKE YOUR HOUSE A *Home*

MADDIE GREER
www.Berouged.com
@maddiegreer

If you had asked me a few years ago what home meant to me, "Nashville, Tennessee," couldn't have fallen quicker from my lips. That all changed in 2014 when I met my husband, Joe, on Instagram. We married in Iceland in 2015, spent 2016 in Portland, Oregon, and eventually moved to New York City in 2017. Traveling has become such a big part of my life since starting my blog that, over the years, living out of a suitcase is a skill I've acquired and mastered.

MY WHY

When it comes to making a home, it's important that I keep it minimal, clean, and sleek with a touch of southern charm. Living in New York City means it's hard to find calm and quiet amid the city noise and busyness, so I strive to create that sense of peace in my home. I love adding vintage pieces here and there, not only because they tell a story but also because they're starting a new one in my home. Being so far from Nashville is never something I will be completely used to, but wherever I am, I will carry my home with me.

FAVORITE TIPS
- Keep it clean and simple.
- Incorporate pieces that are unique and tell a story, things no one else will have.

Motto for Life

I will carry my home with me.

FIVE MUST-HAVES

1 SEATING

People need a place to sit, rest, and talk. Whether you have room for a large sectional or only a couple of chairs, make a plan for seating. Having plenty of seats gives your guests a free pass to relax, and I have also found that people feel more at home when they're sitting. Benches, couches, recliners, ottomans, and even large pillow tufts are great ways to silently say, *Take a seat. You are welcome here.*

The living room's biggest investment will most likely be a quality couch—but don't rush out and buy the first thing you see on sale. Take time to consider what works best for your room's purpose. Here are some things to think through when buying seating:

- *Size:* How large should your piece be to accommodate the size of your family and the number of people you plan to host?
- *Fabric:* Is leather what you need to withstand toddler spills and dog feet? Is cloth more comfortable and affordable? Are slipcover couches something to consider when dirt is inevitable?
- *Comfort:* Is it comfortable? No matter how beautiful the couch, your love for it will quickly fade if no one can relax on it.

Choosing a couch can be tough, especially since there are endless options. As you peruse, make sure you remember your purpose for the space and your functionality needs. Consider your budget and do your research. Putting in time to choose the best fit for your space means you won't have to upgrade in a couple of years, saving you both time and money in the long run.

2 RUG, RUG, RUG

A rug makes it easy to define any space. Because I have an open-concept home and my living room is a part of the kitchen and dining room, designating the sitting area with a rug was important. Rugs are also a great way to make your home feel welcoming and warm. If you have dark floors, play them up with a lighter rug. If you have lighter floors, a pop of color in a rug is a showstopper. If your priority is functionality and you aren't sure what style to use, go with jute. The material fits all styles, comes in many colors, and is super durable.

Bonus: it's *more* than okay to layer a rug over an existing carpet—or another rug. You'd be surprised what adding multiple colors and textures does for a room. Try taking a large

8 x 10-foot jute rug and layering a colorful 5 x 7-foot rug on top.

3 LIGHTING

Lighting brings ambience to any space. If you want to create a homier feel, add table lamps that reflect your style. Using lamps instead of the often-obtrusive overhead lighting creates instant warmth. At night I like to set a quiet, calm mood by turning off our overhead lights and turning on the lamps. The lowered lighting tones down the room and the mood,

encourages the kids to wind down, and makes that transition to bedtime much smoother.

4 PILLOWS

I will never get over the way pillows change a space. I've used pillows to transform many a couch worn out by kids and pets. That instant pop of color will not only add a touch of your personal style, but it can also hide the sagging cushions and stains of a life well lived. Using pillows is the most affordable way (other than paint) to make a space feel new and inviting. You'd be shocked at how many times I've walked past a space and didn't notice anything but the bright, beautiful pillows.

If you're like me, when a new season rolls around, you want to make your space feel fresh. Instead of buying a lot of decorations, simply change your pillows. Of course, having a million bulky pillows to store isn't realistic. I like to buy pillow covers instead. And the best part? They don't take up much space! When you aren't using them, simply flatten and store them in a small bin.

Just don't go overboard! You may think a woman can never have too many pillows, but really, you can. My general rule of thumb is four small pillows for an average, 84-inch couch. If you have too many pillows, you'll run out of room to sit!

5 TABLES

Adding side tables and a coffee table is like adding the belt that pulls your outfit together. Tables provide a resting place for all those things you want visible, such as lamps, fresh flowers, magazines and books about your passions (which make great conversation starters), or even appetizers and drinks for guests. With the right tables, your family and guests will feel right at home.

So how do you find the right ones? You could get matching pieces from a high-end store, but you don't have to. Be creative! There are so many options out there. Instead of a traditional coffee table, use an old trunk with a flat top or an old chicken coop like I did in my she shed (see page 34). If you're wary of repurposing items, I highly encourage you to give it a try. It's amazing how many items I've revamped with just a little paint. Taking on a DIY project can be intimidating at first, so start with a secondhand piece—something that isn't a huge financial investment. That way, if you happen to mess it up, it won't be a big blow to your bank account.

@urbangrayhome

Chapter 3

KITCHEN

My kitchen is for dancing.

The kitchen is for so much more than cooking. In fact, one of my most cherished memories is my mom and dad slow dancing in the kitchen as they prepared dinner. My mom was never a gourmet chef, but it was important to her to create an atmosphere in her kitchen of music, love, conversation, and, of course, food. My parents *still* dance in the kitchen, and now my family dances in the kitchen too. It's a beautiful legacy I hope my children will one day recreate in their own homes. What legacy do you hope to leave your family? Because no matter how big or how tiny your kitchen may be, you have the opportunity to create a space used for greater things than cooking and eating.

> # The kitchen can be more than a place to feed our bodies; it can be a place to feed our souls.

Mom was right when she said food is the way to a man's heart, but the same is true for women and children. We all love to eat, but the kitchen can be more than a place to feed our bodies; it can be a place to feed our souls. By gathering around the warmth of a stove and snatching a sample of whatever is cooking, we build relationships. We celebrate and serve and connect. In the kitchen we have the opportunity to create an atmosphere of trust and to open ourselves to conversations we might otherwise keep inside.

For our family, the kitchen is the central hub, the pit stop, and the heart of our home. Along with the living room, it is the main place we gather. Because we homeschool *and* work from home, our kitchen is always functioning, seldom clean, and rarely empty.

Think about your *why*, that purpose you want your home to fulfill. How can you weave it into the kitchen and in the moments that happen there? What can you do to create an atmosphere that encourages it?

Come, and let's gather in the kitchen.

LAYOUT AND STYLE

When we built our home, I wanted to bring community into our space, so we specifically built our kitchen to be open to the living room. My intention was to allow those cooking (usually me!) to be able to interact with others. You may not have an open-kitchen layout, but don't worry—you can still welcome others in. I've crowded into tiny apartment kitchens, and I've sat at long, luxurious tables. It's not the size or layout of the kitchen that matters most; it's the intention of the heart within it.

Everyone's kitchen is unique, and there's no one perfect layout. Honestly, for most of us, we simply can't change the layout of our kitchen the way we can other rooms. However, we can update the space and add elements to keep it fresh and inviting.

As you look at your kitchen, remember your *why*. What do you want to happen in that space? What can you do to create a warm and inviting gathering space? Consider updating the lighting, painting the cabinets, or simply changing out the cabinet hardware. These things can completely change the atmosphere of your space. You can also spruce up your space with simple and affordable décor items. Pretty dish towels, a decorative clock, and a new rug or runner can make your kitchen feel fresh. And don't forget art that reflects your family's motto. You may not be able to alter your kitchen layout, but you can make simple changes to create a space that's new to you.

Yes, the kitchen is a place to cook, but it's also a place to cultivate a servant's heart, to gather and share precious conversations, and to dance and laugh. It's the heart of the home—not because you share food but because you share love. What will you create in your kitchen?

Stick to Your Style

A lot of homes these days have an open-kitchen layout. Because of this, it's especially important to remember your style should feel cohesive throughout your home. Bring

KEEP IT *Tidy*

Organization and storage are the keys to keeping the kitchen tidy. Add stacking shelves to use the full height of your cabinets. Use drawer organizers for utensils, and toss lids and other loose items into baskets. Keeping clutter off the counters will make the whole room seem cleaner. I know that if my island is clean, I feel like I'm winning!

@abowlfulloflemons

in colors you've used in other rooms. If you don't have an open-concept kitchen, it's still important for your family and guests to feel as if they are transitioning into a like-minded space.

If your kitchen is outdated, use paint to spruce it up. The dark, builder-grade cabinets in our first home made our kitchen look so small. I researched the best paint and tackled the job myself. (If you're interested, I used Glyptex Enamel paint by Porter, recommended by a professional painter. It's not odor-free, but it has held up so well.) I removed all the doors and drawers and laid them out in my garage. It took about a week to paint them, coating each front and back. I cannot tell you the difference it made in our home. A few simple coats of paint brightened up the kitchen and made it look ten times bigger. Consider paint as an inexpensive upgrade.

If you aren't quite ready to paint your cabinets, accessories are a quick and easy way to add a splash of your own personal style. Consider using colors from the rest of your house as accents in your kitchen. Dish towels, vases, and wall art can be used to tie the kitchen to the rest of the house. Lighting, kitchen knobs, faucets, and even coffee stations can reflect the personal style you've chosen to create in the rest of your home.

Style ON A BUDGET

As you look for kitchen décor, don't forget the thrift stores. Scour the aisles to find similar serving pieces, but don't be afraid to mix and match too. A thrifted tiered tray can hold seasonal items, while a vase filled with florals—real or faux—adds a cheerful note.

For paint, be sure to check out the returned paint cans in stores like Lowe's and Home Depot. The "oops" paint, as it's often called, might be just the right color you were looking for—and at significant savings. Just be sure to save the color code on the can's lid. Then, if you need more paint, simply show that code to the staff at the paint desk, and they'll mix up some more.

WHERE TO SHOP

KITCHEN DÉCOR
- Goodwill
- Marshalls
- Pier 1
- T.J.Maxx

CABINET HARDWARE
- Amazon
- Home Depot
- Lowe's

@featherglass

I designed the kitchen with storage in mind but also with the desire to incorporate some French-inspired design elements, like the glass-front pantry with cremone bolts.

@halfwaytoheavenhomestead

To vent hood or not to vent hood, that is the question! After researching, we decided that our answer was *not* to vent hood. If your answer is the same, consider putting a staple piece there for visual interest.

@jaclynjameshome

Adding interesting and unexpected design elements—like subway tile to the ceiling, a bold mosaic tile, or an oversize range hood—is a great way to transform a builder-grade kitchen into a semicustom dream kitchen.

@jesswasserman

Don't be afraid to mix and match styles and textures. In our kitchen we have farmhouse-style cabinets with brass and crystal hardware, faux marble countertops, an old barn workbench we've repurposed as an island, two crystal chandeliers, a 1920s cast iron sink, and a pink Turkish rug. It sounds like a mess, but it fits together really well! Our kitchen feels warm, cozy, and homey.

KILEE NICKELS

www.OneLittleMomma.com
www.NickelandSuede.com
@onelittlemomma

Hi, I'm Kilee. I am a wife, momma, and business owner living outside of Kansas City, Missouri. I love color, but I almost always wear neutrals. I collect cacti and Pendleton beach towels, and my haircut is what most people know me for. My favorite doughnut is lemon-filled, and my preferred drink is milk. Yes, I even order milk at restaurants. At a table full of adults.

In 2014, my husband I started a business called Nickel & Suede, and we've worked together full time ever since! I also write a lifestyle blog called *One Little Momma* where I share my style, ideas, tips, and thoughts with the world. My hope is

that these things inspire women to be the best version of themselves.

MY WHY

As a mom, I feel it's my charge to create a home where love and peace and comfort abound. But it's not easy! I've had to make peace with imperfection as I set the tone for our home. So yes, the painted cabinets have chips and the wood floor has scratches, but the colors are calm, the house is relatively clean, and it's a place where we can play and enjoy each other.

FAVORITE TIPS

- Add plants. Mix real and fake plants to double the effect with half the work. Spend-

ing a little more on the fake plants means your greenery looks very much alive. For real plants, low-maintenance ones such as succulents, snake plants, and cacti make upkeep a breeze.

- Don't be afraid of beige trim! When we moved into our home, I was prepared to paint away all the beige. But thankfully, the budget didn't allow it. The beige trim pairs so well with the white walls and really warms up the palette of our home.

FIVE MUST-HAVES

1 A PLACE TO EAT

Depending on your home, this spot may be inside the kitchen or right outside it. In a tiny loft apartment, it might be a bistro table for two or a few barstools pulled up to an island. It might even be an "empty" spot next to a counter where your friend can lean while you cook and talk. Give yourself somewhere for conversation, rest, and a bit of eating.

2 SERVING PIECES

Treat yourself (and your guests) to a beautiful serving platter, an antique teapot, or a special wine glass. It makes cooking and dining much more enjoyable—and that means a lot coming from someone who hates to cook!

3 A DRINK STATION

If you are going to drink coffee or tea, make your life easier by displaying your equipment. This doesn't have to be a big ordeal. I have a small mug rack and my Keurig sitting out, along with a drawer full of coffees and teas. I can't tell you the number of guests who have commented on my station. It's a sweet surprise and so easy to create. Check out my friend Angela's coffee bar (@angelarose_diyhome; see page 47). What a unique space she's created! Doesn't it make you crave a cup of coffee?

4 YES, A RUG!

It may seem odd to have a rug in the kitchen, but I can't tell you how much warmer and welcoming a rug makes your kitchen feel. I have a long runner behind my island, and it's so nice on my feet as I'm washing those endless dishes. You may find a simple runner

works best in your space, or perhaps a small round rug under a table is better. I'll say it again: rugs define spaces and create visual interest. And don't worry about the inevitable spills—vacuums were invented to clean up crumbs. And most any stain can be defeated by the wealth of stain-fighting information on the internet.

5 A DROP ZONE

The kitchen ends up holding way more than food. Mail, loose change, papers, keys, phone chargers, sunglasses—they all seem to land here, so it's nice to have a designated spot for these items. We use a simple mason jar for change, a cute basket for keys, and a designated drawer for sunglasses and extra chargers. Consider also hanging a paper organizer or calendar nearby for easy access to the day's tasks.

@angelarose_diyhome

Chapter 4

DINING ROOM

The table is where food is shared, conversations are collected, and hearts are gathered together.

Four months after we moved into our new home, we invited a group of friends over. Fifteen people were seated semicomfortably around my dining table, and I remember pausing to take a mental picture and thinking, *This is what you wanted.* Looking at each face, watching each smile, hearing each laugh . . . it was the moment I had dreamed of when I found my barnwood table months before and then while I painted and restored the old church pew. Seeing those faces and sharing a meal together was the very thing I had waited so long for. My *why*, my purpose, became a reality, and what a sweet one it was.

The dining room is a space to grow together as you share life and create memories.

The dining room or dining area is a place to sit, converse, and (of course) eat. It is also a space to grow together as you share life and create memories. You don't have to have a formal dining room either. It can be any area where you gather for a meal and conversation.

If your family is anything like ours, the dining room, especially the dining room table, is used for much more than dinner. It's where Easter eggs are dyed and Yahtzee and chess are played. Schoolwork happens here daily. It's the spot for endless coloring sessions, for laundry sorting, and occasionally, for eating. Our dining room is one of the most used spaces in our home.

What about yours? What's your *why* for this space? What purpose do you want your dining area to serve? How many different things happen in your dining space? And how can you be intentional about using that space to meet your needs?

Come and join me in the dining room.

LAYOUT AND STYLE

Begin by looking at the space you have available. Do you have an island with stools, an eat-in kitchen nook, or a separate dining room? Which space do you use most for actual eating? Our home has a small kitchen nook with a round table that seats about four, and we also have a dining "room" as a part of the living room that holds our farmhouse table and comfortably seats twelve. Once you've identified your space (or spaces), consider the pieces you need to accomplish your purpose for the space.

Obviously, you'll need a table that fits both your style and your purpose. (I talk more about how to choose the right one on page 61.)

Also consider a buffet or hutch to hold extra food and dishes for entertaining and to store seasonal items. If you have space, it's nice to be able to store your "good" china or those seldom-used, large glass bowls out of the way but still within easy reach. Buffets and hutches come in all design styles and can fit any home. First consider the items you have and if you would like them to be displayed. This will help you decide whether you should choose a hutch or a buffet. If you serve meals regularly and appreciate the presentation, a buffet is a great option for laying out the food buffet-style. If you enjoy collecting dishes, consider a hutch with an open or glass front that would allow them to be displayed.

I love collecting white dishes of any size and shape. I have mine displayed in our antique 1890s hutch. In the closed cabinets, I store my kids' art supplies and games—because we often play around the table too. It's also where I store extra seasonal items like table runners and napkins.

A hutch can be pretty and practical. If you're drawn to this piece and it works for your needs, add it to your dining space. But if it doesn't work for your home, don't force it. It's better to have enough room to move about easily. Consider your purpose for the space before making this large purchase.

Bonus tip: Besides regular dusting, once every six months I take all my dishes from the hutch and run them through the dishwasher. While they're washing, I deep clean the hutch

KEEP IT *Tidy*

If you stick to a neutral dinner plate, then you only need a collection of dessert or salad plates, runners, and napkins for each season. And this means you have fewer items to store because they don't take up much space! Designate a shelf in your pantry, a spot in an old hutch, or a drawer in your china cabinet for storage. I like to stash my napkins and runners in baskets in my hutch. This is a simple way to turn storage into a pretty display.

@ourvictorianitaliante

shelves. When it's time to put the dishes back, I don't put them in the same spot they came from. Changing things up a bit makes the space feel fresh and new.

Decorating the Table

The table is, of course, the focal point of the dining room, so decorating it is key. There are two main ways I do this. The first—and the easiest—is to simply add a centerpiece. It adds a touch of your personal style but also allows the majority of the surface to be open for use. A centerpiece can be a display of candles, a vase with florals, garland, or even small trees at Christmas. It can be a seasonal display that you change often, or it can be a neutral display that stays out year-round. The possibilities are endless and completely up to you. Find inspiration in store displays, friends' homes, and your own imagination. A good rule of thumb is to use a lighter-color table runner under your centerpiece to add a pop of texture and color and to anchor your centerpiece in the space.

@handmade.farmhouse

You don't have to spend a fortune to decorate while entertaining. When I create table-scapes, I love to gather beautiful pieces from outside. Fresh herbs, garden blooms, and branch clippings make the centerpiece feel special and unique.

@bigfamilylittlefarmhouse

The second way to decorate your table is called *tablescaping*. It means actually setting your table—artistically—place by place. You can add as much or as little detail as you like. You are the artist! Keep in mind that while tablescaping is beautiful, it isn't necessarily practical if you use the space daily for meals. Because we rarely use the table in our kitchen nook for eating, this is the one I use for tablescaping. If I were to tablescape my dining table—which is in constant use—I would be forever moving and rearranging the décor. So the dining table gets decorated only for special holidays and dinners.

Tablescaping can be really fun, and it's one of my favorite ways to decorate. You can change your table décor for seasons and holidays or for different types of get-togethers. If this sounds appealing to you, consider purchasing a plate of solid color. I chose a white

plate that can be used year-round. Second, buy chargers or placemats to set the plate on. These can easily be switched out for the different seasons. Or choose a neutral placemat to use year-round and change out your napkins for color. Next, add a salad plate. It can be white also, or it can be a seasonal color or pattern. Top with a decorative item in the center of your plates. This can be a napkin ring, a Christmas ornament, a piece of faux fruit, or whatever you like. The possibilities are endless. Choose items that complement your centerpiece. For example, if my floral-garland centerpiece has red berries, I'll add a red napkin or napkin ring. If I am using burgundy and fall florals as a centerpiece, then I might use jewel-toned scarves for table runners, using the same colors for napkins as well.

My biggest tip when shopping is to find one item that speaks to you, that item you just *absolutely* fall in love with. For me, it was a scarf in the colors of fall. I pulled its colors into the chargers, the napkins, and my giant florals. Inside the center of my plates, I placed a faux apple to bring out the same burgundy as in the scarf. Finish off your tablescape with your favorite utensils and glasses, and you'll have created a beautiful table.

The dining area—whether it's a table or a whole room—offers a designated spot to focus your decorating efforts on each holiday season. If that seems like too much work for your taste, find one centerpiece you love and simply change out the florals as needed. Always remember your *why* and let that be your guide for decorating.

Style ON A BUDGET

Hobby Lobby is my go-to for staying on budget for dining room décor. They have wonderfully affordable chargers for $1.99. They also have quality white plates, which can be used for each season, saving you money and storage space. Creating a different look is as simple as changing out the napkins. That's what I do!

WHERE TO SHOP

PLATES, NAPKINS, AND SEASONAL DÉCOR
- Hobby Lobby
- T.J.Maxx

TABLES: SECONDHAND DEALS
- Facebook Marketplace
- OfferUp
- VarageSale

@bigfamilylittlefarmhouse

One of the busiest rooms in our home, our dining room sees everything from family dinners to homeschool projects to our three-year-old's latest car collection! Simplicity and organization help us maintain a space that is beautiful but functional at the same time. Baskets to hide toys are a great way to keep your kiddos happy while maintaining the style that you love.

@exceeding.joy

Secondhand, mismatched chairs are a great way to give an eclectic look for little money.

@finding_lovely

Sometimes the best design features are windows. Natural light adds so much to a space. When designing the kitchen, I paid close attention to the windows, adding this window-seat nook to give interest and light to the space.

@threesonsfarmhouse

Creating a beautiful space doesn't need to be hard on your wallet. Shopping at places like Goodwill for rugs (like the jute rug pictured here) or utilizing apps like OfferUp (where I found this farmhouse table for $100) allows you to build a space on a budget. Saving money when you can may help you feel more at ease when you need to splurge on statement pieces, such as these salvaged LA school chairs found at a local vintage market.

MAKE YOUR HOUSE A *Home*

KARAN BARTON
www.DesignsbyKaran.com
@designsbykaran

A crooked path led me to design. Although I have always loved it, my background is in early childhood education and social work. Surprisingly, my training as a counselor has come in handy with my design clients. Who would have thought designing homes would require counseling skills? (And if you haven't guessed, my sense of humor is very dry.) I started my own design company, Inside Out Designs, in Ontario, Canada, in 2007, and I'm happiest with a paintbrush in my hand or a design plan in front of me.

In my designs I reuse and upcycle pieces and create homes unique to those living in them. In my own home I wanted my main entrance to feel welcoming and inviting. I worked hard to create a kitchen that enables anyone to be a part of the conversations going on in the room. And right off the kitchen, the sunroom is a cozy and relaxed space we use often.

MY WHY
For me, family is everything. And to "live with love; walk in grace" is something we are all aiming for. I am a designer and social media influencer because it enables me to create homes that welcome people in, encourage them to put their feet up, and provide a safe place to just be.

Motto for Life
Live with love; walk in grace.

At some point, my Instagram account became more than just a place to share my designs—I've found a group of strong, fierce, and encouraging women there. As a cancer survivor, I've learned to seize each day and to support others in their endeavors, knowing we rise by lifting others up. So I encourage you, no matter your age, to go after your dreams. It's never too late to discover something new about yourself. Life is too short to do something that doesn't make your heart content. When you are happy, that happiness spreads, and you become someone who encourages, supports, and helps others follow their dreams.

FAVORITE TIPS

- Use pieces you love, not whatever is on trend or what everyone else is using.
- Always design your space according to *your* family's needs.
- Choose colors you find soothing and make you happy.

FIVE MUST-HAVES

1 THE TABLE

Having a table is essential, of course, but think about which activities might happen at that table.

- Will it be a formal, only-for-eating spot, or will you use it for homework and craft projects too?
- Do you want family meals in the kitchen nook?
- Do you want to host a dinner party of fifteen in your formal dining space, or would you rather sit on the floor with pillows around a large coffee table in your apartment?

Also, think about what kind of hosting you want to do, how many family members eat there regularly, and what kind of atmosphere you want to create. Knowing your purpose will help you pick the right table. Here are some important questions to consider before purchasing a table:

- What is the square footage of your space? What size table will fit there?
- Would a round table work better than a rectangular one?
- What is your design style? Your table will be a reflection of your style based on material and finish. For example, if

you love rustic, consider natural wood or barnwood in a farmhouse-style table. For traditional, go with dark, rich wood tones in a classic oval or rectangular shape. Modern would lean more toward sleek lines, perhaps with glass and metal accents, while eclectic can be simply whatever you love.

- How many chairs do you need for your family?
- Do you entertain regularly? Would you benefit from a table that extends for additional seating?

Of course, the budget will affect your decisions too. Does your budget allow you to shop for something new? Or would a thrifted or slightly used piece work better? Or perhaps you can give your mom's hand-me-down table a paint job. It doesn't have to be new to create a whole new look for you.

2 A PLACE TO SIT

Because your dining area will see a lot of traffic, choose seating that will hold up, like wood or metal.. But make sure it's comfortable—after all, this is a place you want to gather and linger. You'll also want your seating to reflect the overall style and functionality

@oldsaltfarm

of your home. Do you want a modern chair that's clear acrylic or a sleek black chair to go with your boho vibe? Perhaps you prefer a more traditional chair, even something that's upholstered. Or do you need something wipeable for children (and clumsy adults)?

Keep in mind that chairs don't have to match either. My dining area has half a church pew on one side and a row of wooden chairs on the other. An eclectic group of chairs in a similar tone works beautifully. Painting an old set white can also be completely charming.

3 YES, A RUG HERE TOO!

Does the recommendation to add a rug surprise you? Yes, even in the dining area, a rug can help define the space. I know people have differing opinions about this. I can hear one of my grandmothers saying now, "Why on earth you would want a rug under a place you eat?" On the flip side, I can see my other grandmother's entire dining room suite set atop a plush white carpet. To each her own, right? While I personally don't have a rug under my dining space—it would have to be big enough to accommodate my 10-foot-long table—the trend now is to use a rug. (And I do have one under my kitchen nook table.) If you decide to add a rug, use one that brings in the colors from other areas in your home. It should be big enough to extend beyond your chairs about a foot or so. This allows the rug to look big enough for your space and confines your furniture. When in doubt, jute is a wonderful option here too. It's durable and easy to vacuum.

4 PLACE SETTINGS

There's something special about a set table, whether you make a beautiful arrangement just for dinner or you leave it out for a tablescape year-round. First, design your place settings around your family's needs. In general, I recommend purchasing eight interchangeable place settings with neutral placemats. Use a white dinner plate and invest in colorful or seasonal salad plates. Stack your items to add height, layering the placemat, dinner plate, and salad plate, then adding a napkin and napkin ring on top. Place glasses and silverware beside each place setting. Add candles for a touch of warmth and elegant coziness. Once the table is decorated, your family and friends will love the special touch, and it will create such sweet memories.

5 DÉCOR

The dining table is one of the main places I decorate in my home. A pretty table sets the mood for the experience to come. Whether it's simply fresh flowers in the center or a lavish tablescape, a decorated table provides a beautiful focal point for your room. Consider

@thetailoredhaven

investing in neutral vases or bowls you can use every season. These allow you to quickly change the contents to reflect the season or a special occasion. If you prefer to leave your décor on the table while eating, try to keep it below eye level. Use small vases of fresh flowers or low candles. I remove my large centerpiece when dining because it obstructs the view and hinders the natural flow of conversation.

Restful Places

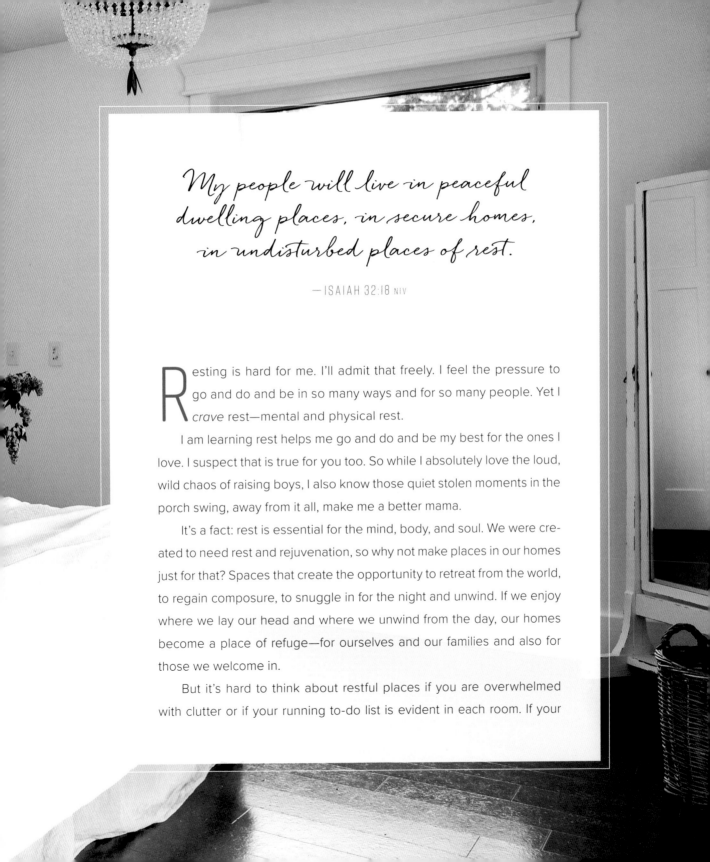

*My people will live in peaceful
dwelling places, in secure homes,
in undisturbed places of rest.*

—ISAIAH 32:18 NIV

Resting is hard for me. I'll admit that freely. I feel the pressure to go and do and be in so many ways and for so many people. Yet I *crave* rest—mental and physical rest.

I am learning rest helps me go and do and be my best for the ones I love. I suspect that is true for you too. So while I absolutely love the loud, wild chaos of raising boys, I also know those quiet stolen moments in the porch swing, away from it all, make me a better mama.

It's a fact: rest is essential for the mind, body, and soul. We were created to need rest and rejuvenation, so why not make places in our homes just for that? Spaces that create the opportunity to retreat from the world, to regain composure, to snuggle in for the night and unwind. If we enjoy where we lay our head and where we unwind from the day, our homes become a place of refuge—for ourselves and our families and also for those we welcome in.

But it's hard to think about restful places if you are overwhelmed with clutter or if your running to-do list is evident in each room. If your

We were created to need rest and rejuvenation, so why not make places in our homes just for that?

home feels far from restful, choose the areas that could provide the most rest and visualize what could bring calm to those spaces. Do you need to purge some items, or do you need one designated space for working on projects so other areas can be used solely for relaxing? Then consider what extra touches you could add to create a deeply restful place.

Throughout our home I try to create an atmosphere of rest. Aesthetically that happens with softly textured throws and pillows and with the gentle lighting of side table lamps. The sweet, fragrant smells of essential oils, such as lavender and orange, encourage a sense of peace and calm. I continue that restful theme outside, where rocking chairs invite us to sit on the porch, relax a while, and enjoy the view.

As you seek to create these restful places in your home, pause for a few moments to ponder these questions:

- What does rest look like for you and your family? Is it curling up alone with a book? Or is it gathering with loved ones around a crackling firepit?
- Do you have areas in your home that are already restful? What contributes to that restful feeling?
- Where would you like to create a more restful space?
- Is there a particular fragrance that your family loves that could help create a sense of peace and calm?

Now gather your answers, and let's create your restful places together.

Chapter 5

MASTER BEDROOM

*In peace I will lie down and sleep, for you
alone, O Lord, will keep me safe.*

—PSALM 4:8 NLT

The master bedroom should be your haven, a home within the home. It is the one place, above all others, that should feel genuinely and completely *yours*—your zone, your space—because the bedroom is more than simply a place to sleep. It is your sanctuary and your retreat. It's where thoughts are carried into dreams and where each new day is ushered in.

The bedroom is where thoughts are carried into dreams.

This room is the most intimate space in the home, yet so many of us leave it untouched. We don't make it a priority, because we claim no one sees it but us, and it's easy to shut away the mess. But I believe the opposite is true. Because the bedroom is where you go to relax and retreat, it should be a priority. It doesn't have to be a designer showroom, but it should be comfortable, and it should embody who you are.

To create my own bedroom retreat, I focused on the bed. Because it is the focal point of the room, I think it should get the most attention. I splurged on the bedding, choosing linens that looked and felt luxurious. By layering textures with an added quilt and dreamy pillows, the bed invites me to lie down, sink in, and rest from the cares of the world. Soft lighting created by bedside lamps enhances the restful atmosphere. When your

bedroom beckons you to relax, you'll know you've met your goal of a restful place.

So let's create your own retreat.

LAYOUT AND STYLE

The basic components of a bedroom are largely the same for everyone. You will, of course, need a bed. You also may need a dresser for storage and nightstands for holding phones, books, and that middle-of-the-night glass of water. I like to look for the largest wall or the wall that faces the door and put the bed there. It's often more appealing to see the bed upon entering a room. Next, place your other furniture pieces.

As you consider layout, make sure this room serves your *why*. For example, let's say that reading is important to you. If so, try to incorporate a reading chair into your layout. In general, though, I've found that sticking to a few key furniture pieces is best. Cluttering a room with too many pieces makes it less inviting and not as easy to relax in.

What about color and style? Do you want this room to flow with the rest of your home? Or do you want this room to be something unique? There are so many options when designing a bedroom. My first piece of advice is to think about the cohesive look you are

creating throughout the rest of your home. If you are designing your master and have a modern home, incorporate this style into your bedroom choices. Choose a bed that's metal or wood with sleek lines. Platform beds or sleek, four-poster canopy beds work well for a modern home. If you've chosen a farm-house style, then think natural wood tones and neutral palettes. For a traditional style, stick to matching bedside tables and classic wood tones. An eclectic style can be achieved by integrating treasured furniture pieces along with a colorful rug, favorite art prints or pictures, or an indoor plant in the corner of your room.

Incorporate linens that reflect the colors and tones you've chosen in the rest of the house. Duvets are a great way to do this. Not only are they affordable pieces, but they can be easily changed when it's time for a refresh. First, choose your duvet insert. Next, find the duvet cover that works with your taste and style. I personally like to use solid neutrals and add accent colors with a fun throw or quilt at the end of the bed, along with some throw pillows at the head.

Curtains are a lovely way to add style and color as well as privacy. If your bedspread is a solid color, it's more than okay to choose curtains with patterns and texture. If your bedspread is loud and colorful, sticking to a solid-colored curtain is a great way to balance out your room. And no matter your style, you can elongate your windows and give the illusion of higher ceilings by hanging your curtains up to a foot above your windows.

KEEP IT *Tidy*

To create a feeling of peace and tranquility, get rid of clutter in the bedroom. Because many homes don't have walk-in closets, extra storage is always a plus. Rolling, under-the-bed storage bins are perfect for storing shoes or off-season clothes. Consider buying nightstands with a drawer or two to serve as mini-dressers to hold socks, skivvies, or other items. Keep a laundry basket in the bathroom or closet to catch dirty clothes. Consider keeping your jewelry and other accessories organized and near where you dress. This eliminates the need to leave some items in the closet, some on the dresser, and some on the bathroom counter. In the closet, hang a corkboard in a pretty frame to hold necklaces and bracelets. A fancy curtain rod attached to the closet wall is perfect for draping scarves, and switching those old shoe boxes for clear storage bins will help you see what's inside and create a more organized space. I have found when I designate a place for each of my things, I'm more likely to keep my space clean and tidy—and thus, more restful.

@abowlfulloflemons

Even though my ceilings are higher, I still hang my curtains five to ten inches above the windows.

Once you've settled on your layout and design, it's time to roll up your sleeves and get ready to relax.

Rest is essential for our lives, yet we often neglect the room for doing just that. Make your rest a priority and fulfill your *why* for this space. Because at the end of the day, when all is said and done, you should be able to walk into your bedroom and find . . . *rest*.

Style ON A BUDGET

Need a mattress? Use the bed in a box on Amazon! The Zinus brand is one of our favorites because they have the greatest memory foam mattresses. In fact, we have them in every bedroom in our house, even our camper, and we wouldn't use anything else. Don't spend thousands on a mattress. Spend $250 or less, get it delivered to your door, and sleep *great*.

WHERE TO SHOP

LINENS
- LinensandHutch.com*
- T.J.Maxx

CURTAINS
- IKEA (My favorite!)
- Pier 1
- T.J.Maxx
- Wayfair

BEDS AND OTHER FURNITURE
- Facebook Marketplace
- IKEA
- T.J.Maxx
- Walmart
- Wayfair

*Use my code CRATEANDCOTTAGE for 30% off.

MAKE YOUR HOUSE A *Home*

ANITA YOKOTA
www.AnitaYokota.com
@anitayokota

Hi, I'm the designer behind the interior design blog at AnitaYokota.com. Growing up in a second-generation Asian American home, I spent countless hours looking at my mom's collection of *Better Homes & Gardens* magazines, and I rearranged my family's furniture constantly. I loved to pretend the room I shared with my sister was a New York City loft apartment.

My passion for interior styling continued to grow as I entered adulthood. Eventually, I started an Instagram account and a blog where I offer on-trend design tips that can be translated to any home. Each tip is broken down into simple steps so that anyone—no matter what level of experience—can follow them!

Why? Because we love teaching our three young daughters the importance of being kind and humble yet strong enough to stand up for what is right.

MY WHY
I view my home as our haven. I love creating functional, cozy, and inviting spaces for my family to enjoy. We spend a lot of time at home making memories and creating special moments together, so it is important for our home to be as meaningful and comfortable as possible while still being functional.

When our daughters were younger, our master bedroom was the drop zone for toys, clutter, and unfolded laundry. Now, it is a place for my husband and I to relax and unwind after a busy day.

FAVORITE TIPS

- I love mixing neutrals and color together. Alternating these palettes through pillows, furniture, textiles, and art creates a balanced and effortless look.

- Invest in a piece you really love rather than just buying something (or a whole bunch of somethings) to fill up a space. If that means waiting and saving up for a higher-end piece of furniture, do that! Striking a balance between high-end furniture and affordable accent pieces is a great way to round out the look of a room.

@angelarose_diyhome

@featherglass

A light, neutral color makes for a serene space you can retreat to at the end of the day, and texture on the walls and ceiling gives an extra cozy feel. Add a few accessories to make your space even more appealing.

Since the master bedroom was a new addition to an old house, I incorporated the antique marble fireplace and antique glass transom windows to keep the room from feeling like a new build.

@selah.pines.farmhouse

Don't forget to use a corner to create a sweet spot to sip a cup of coffee while enjoying a comfy pillow. Some natural light is always a bonus.

@keely.mann

You will never go wrong with adding pops of pink!

MAKE YOUR HOUSE A *Home*

JODIE KAMMERER & JULIE LANCIA, THE DESIGN TWINS

www.TheDesignTwins.com
@jodie.thedesigntwins & @julie.thedesigntwins

We are identical twins and best friends, and while we live separately—Julie in Seattle and Jodie in San Francisco— our work brings us together. We are writers, decorators, DIYers, bloggers, and Instagram influencers. But that's not all! We are also classically trained violinists, are bilingual in French, and both have our master's degrees in education. We have taught many things: English as a second language, French, violin, scrapbooking, personal style, and decorating. Now we organize and teach our own Instagram workshops.

OUR WHY

More than anything, we love helping others. Since the beginning of our journey, our *why* has been deeply rooted in our desire to connect with people in personal, meaningful ways and to inspire them to find joy. We are passionate about teaching and encouraging others to express themselves creatively. On Instagram and on our blog, *The Design Twins*, we strive to inspire people to live their best lives by becoming the best version of themselves. To us, decorating is much more art than science. Our goal is to

help people find and articulate their personal style and empower them to enjoy the process.

FAVORITE TIPS

- Go natural. No matter your style, it's hard to go wrong if you stick to elements inspired by nature.
- Choose a color scheme and stick to it. There's nothing worse than a hodgepodge of random colors.
- Symmetry (i.e., arranging pieces on either side of a focal point to create balance) is an easy and universally appealing way to create harmony in a space.

FIVE MUST-HAVES

1 A BED

Consider the size. Do you only have room for a double? Or would a king-size bed better fit you and your snoring husband—and that child who never seems to stay in his own bed? When it comes to creating a beautiful sleeping area, there are lots of options. Craft your own headboard with a DIY project, or simply buy a metal frame and dress up the wall behind it with paint or board-and-batten.

2 DRESSERS AND NIGHTSTANDS

Gone are the days of matching bedroom suites, so don't be afraid to think outside the box. Mix and match pieces for a more eclectic look. Pair a new console table with an old desk. Check out Pinterest for some wonderful hacks for elevating IKEA dressers and nightstands, such as these nightstands by @whitesparrowfarm. By adding trim and decorative feet (which you can buy on places like Etsy), you can transform drab pieces into fabulous finds that fit your style. End tables make great nightstands for holding lamps, books, and late-night snacks.

3 A RUG OR TWO

Yes, put a rug down. Define that space for your bed. Even placing a rug at the foot of a bed can be so pleasing to the eye. I like to place the rug halfway under the bed so that it sticks out a few feet or more from the end of the bed itself. That pop of color and texture creates a warmer atmosphere and a pleasing feeling under your feet.

4 BEDDING AND PILLOWS

Dare to go beyond buying a bed in a

@whitesparrowfarm

@whitesparrowfarm

bag. Start with a neutral quilt or comforter, and dress it up with pillows or simple white shams. Duvet covers make it easy to refresh any space. Find what you like and go with it. Adding a bed skirt allows you to hide storage items under your bed—and those pesky dust bunnies!

5 **LIGHTING**

Perhaps more than any other room, lighting is so important in the bedroom. Give yourself ambiance with low side table lamps. Or if you're really adventurous, change that fan light for a dimmable chandelier. It can be done—let YouTube be your teacher!

Chapter 6

BATHROOM

Wash your troubles away.

The bathroom can be so much more than a place to shower or brush your teeth. With just a few touches, it can be transformed into a wonderful escape. And why not? After all, it's the place where we prepare to face the world and then wash away the stresses of the day. The bathroom is where we think our morning thoughts and our bedtime wishes. It's where we look in the mirror, gather our confidence, and decide that, yes, we can do this all again today. And if you're a parent, the bathroom may be your only place of escape and solace. (Although shutting the door doesn't seem to prevent their tiny fingers from wiggling underneath!)

The bathroom is where we think our morning thoughts and our bedtime wishes.

Make your bathroom a place of retreat, an oasis of calm and peace. For myself, I indulged in an elegant clawfoot tub that's perfect for soaking away the cares of the world. Luxurious towels and a soft, colorful rug make me feel completely pampered. Don't be afraid to indulge yourself a bit too. Invest in those extra-soft, just-the-right-color bath towels. If soaking in a bath helps you unwind, buy those bath salts you've been wanting to try. Display them in a pretty basket or glass jar so when you walk in, you're reminded of their promise to escape, rest, and retreat.

So come, and let's talk about creating your own oasis.

LAYOUT AND STYLE

When it comes to the layout of the bathroom, it's often a case of "what you see is what you get." With all the plumbing, you can't rearrange a bathroom without gutting it, and that quickly gets expensive. The basic elements of bathrooms are essentially the same: some sort of tub or shower, a toilet, and a vanity area. And while the layout isn't easily changed, there are things you can do to transform the space.

Update your vanity with a fresh coat of paint to match the rest of the house. Add a wall shelf or corner shelf to hold towels and décor. Bring in a rug or runner that isn't made for bathrooms. People assume you need the fuzzy nonslip rugs, but try using a stylish rug from another area of your home and see how polished this room becomes (just add a bit of rug tape). And hanging art on the wall is more than okay in a bathroom. We spend a lot of time here, so why not make it beautiful?

Painting the walls or redoing the flooring are options that don't require breaking the bank, especially when you choose to do the labor yourself. If you have an outdated bathroom, try painting the tiles or stenciling the flooring. Bring in colors from your bedroom or other areas of the house with towels, paint

color, and accessories to keep it cohesive. Even if DIY isn't your thing, changing towels, rugs, window treatments, and shower curtains can make a huge difference. Make the scene more relaxing by lighting candles in your favorite scent and playing some quiet music.

With today's endless options, it's easy to bring your own sense of style and color into the bath. Just a few simple and intentional changes can transform this space into one of your favorite places to relax, refresh, and rejuvenate.

Style ON A BUDGET

Use metallic spray paint to refresh existing light fixtures, plumbing fixtures, towel rods, knobs, and toilet paper holders. There are an incredible number of spray paint colors and finishes available these days, and this simple update makes the room feel new.

WHERE TO SHOP

VANITIES
- Habitat for Humanity ReStore
- Home Depot
- Lowe's

LIGHTING
- Amazon
- Antique Farmhouse
- Home Depot
- Lowe's

HARDWARE, FIXTURES, AND ACCESSORIES
- Habitat for Humanity ReStore
- Home Depot
- Lowe's
- T.J.Maxx

@angelarose_diyhome

Warm wood tones combined with bright white walls give a spa-like feel. When other elements are kept simple, a fun, patterned floor tile adds interest without being overwhelming.

@bryartonfarm

The key to making a new vanity look old is in the finishes. To give the room a little age, we added cast iron hardware, an antique-style faucet, and a hand-carved backsplash to a marble-topped vanity.

MAKE YOUR HOUSE A *Home*

ASHLEY PETRONE
www.ArrowsandBow.com
@arrowsandbow

My name is Ashley Petrone. A few years ago I was a stay-at-home mom with a passion for creativity. After years of homeschooling my kids, I decided to pursue my passion and start a blog. I knew hardly anything about the social media space, but that didn't stop me—I just went for it! About seven months in, my family and I had the opportunity to buy land and eventually build a house. We decided to take the leap and sell our five-bedroom, 2,800-square-foot home. Not only did we take the leap, but we also made a big splash! We sold everything we owned, bought a 180-square-foot RV, renovated it, and moved our family of five into it and lived on our land.

MY WHY
Living in our RV was life-changing. It taught us we didn't need much, gave us an appreciation for the things we had but took for granted, and brought us together as a family. Our lives quickly stopped being about building our dream home and became about finding joy in this in-between. Because of a job transfer, we spent seventeen months in the RV before moving into a home. We never built our dream home, but that motto of finding joy in every moment still holds true.

Motto for Life
Find joy in the in-between.

We have since purchased a 1,300-square-foot home in Northern California and have had so much fun renovating it. We're slowly adding in things we love, choosing everything with intention and remembering the lessons in simplicity from our time in the RV.

FAVORITE TIPS

- Only keep things you love and use.
- Want a quick room update? Paint! It's my favorite way to refresh my home.

FIVE MUST-HAVES

1 PAINT

If your bathroom is small, paint it a light and bright color. My go-to color is Repose Gray by Sherwin-Williams (we've used it on almost every square inch of our interior and have not been disappointed). A light color allows you to play with bolder patterns and colors in your décor. And did you know you can transform those old '60s pink-and-blue-tiled bathrooms with epoxy paint? You can paint practically anything these days, and it's a cheap way to make a space look on trend with your design style.

2 VANITY CABINETS

If you're unhappy with the look of your vanity cabinets, consider painting them. Or replace the vanity entirely. Check out the before and after of Stacey's bathroom renovation (@farmhousechic4sure). If you're really daring, you can try using an old dresser for your vanity instead. Just make sure you find a piece that can house the plumbing underneath. I used my grandmother's old wash stand (see page 86). We purchased the sink bowl and faucet on Amazon. If you're willing to

Left: before

Below: after renovation

@farmhousechic4sure

@whitesparrowfarm

ter lights for hanging pendant lighting—they even make kits for this! Or perhaps hang a chandelier. (Check the building codes for your state first!) Do it yourself using YouTube as a guide, always making sure the electricity is turned off, of course. If working with wiring is a little intimidating, hire an electrician to do it for you.

4 FLOORING

If you're unhappy with your flooring, change it. New tile or flooring may not be in your budget, but there are many stylish linoleum options. Some will stick right on top of your existing linoleum. Consider stenciling or painting over your existing tile. Paint with an epoxy tile paint and then add a fun floor stencil on top. Etsy and Home Depot are great resources for stencils. You just have to take the plunge.

5 FIXTURES AND ACCESSORIES

Update cabinet knobs, towel bars, and toilet paper holders. These are all small jobs you can do yourself easily and inexpensively. If you're ready to try something a bit bigger, replace your faucets. (Remember, YouTube can teach you practically anything!) Simply adding new towels, bath rugs, a shower curtain, and candles can completely transform your space.

think outside the box, changing up your vanity doesn't have to break the bank.

3 LIGHTING

Updating the lighting can completely transform a bathroom. Change that builder-grade vanity lighting to something more your style. Often, it's as simple as unscrewing the old and attaching the new. Switch out canis-

Chapter 7

GUEST ROOM

*Warmly welcome each other . . . just as
Christ has warmly welcomed you.*

—ROMANS 15:7 TLB

I have a friend who always creates an inviting space when we come over. Our beds are perfectly made. The side table lamps are lit, and fresh flowers adorn the room. A welcome basket awaits us with bottled waters, tissues, and other small toiletries. Fresh towels are folded on the bathroom counter, and pretty bottles of soap and shampoo are thoughtfully provided. These are all such simple touches, yet they make us feel thought of, welcomed, and ready to relax from our journey.

Whether you come in to visit or just to rest, when you enter our home, may you be blessed.

Having a guest room is very important to some homeowners. Because we have family who visit on a regular basis, having a guest room is a necessity for us. Do you often have overnight guests? If so, you'll want to create a space for them to not only rest in but retreat to. Ensuring your guests have a few basic amenities is really all you need to make sure their stay is comfortable. A bed, an empty drawer or section in a closet for hanging clothes, and an end table or two with lamps will make your guests feel welcome and at home.

If you don't have a designated space for guests but still need one occasionally, you might want to purchase a pullout couch for your living room or bonus area. Or consider putting a queen-size bed in one of your children's rooms. That way, when guests come, you can give your guests the bed and let the kids "pallet it out" on the living room floor.

So come, and let's make a place for your guests.

LAYOUT AND STYLE

As with any other room, the guest room should fit the needs of those using it. Ask yourself these questions:

- Who are the guests who will regularly use your space?
- Do they have special needs you might need to accommodate?
- Do you have space for a dedicated guest room? If not, investing in a sleeper sofa or a well-made air mattress might be the way to go.
- Will this space be used only for a guest room, or will it serve other purposes as well?
- Do your guests need space in a closet or an armoire for hanging clothes? Or an empty drawer in a dresser?
- Do they need nightstands to hold lamps, books, and other miscellaneous items?
- Is there ready access to a bathroom, fresh towels, and other necessities?

@white.farmhouse

who is visiting. For example, if an elderly couple is visiting and you have a bedroom on the main floor, consider making this their space so they don't have to navigate the stairs. If you have a family with children visiting, let the kids have a slumber party in the living room while the grown-ups take the kids' room for the night. I've found that kids can sleep most anywhere, and giving your guests a space they can close off creates more privacy.

If you're in a small apartment or home, consider what area might be best for your guests. That may mean giving up your own room so that they have a comfortable place to sleep with a bit of privacy. Or it could mean rearranging some furniture in a living room for ideal comfort and space. For extra sleeping

Once you know your purpose for the space and the guests you'll accommodate, layouts for guest rooms are simple. All you need is a bed and somewhere guests can put their belongings. Treat this room (or space) much like you would any other room in the house. Design it with your colors and style as well as the comfort of your guests in mind. If necessary, change your accommodations based on

KEEP IT *Tidy*

Keeping the guest area tidy is more about the things you do as you prepare for guests to arrive. Setting out clean sheets and towels, switching on a bedside lamp, and clearing away an area for unpacking is a great way to prepare for your guests.

accommodations and to save space when you don't have guests, purchase an air mattress and invest in a memory foam mattress topper for extra comfort. We have two of these at our house and have used them on countless occasions.

As with other rooms, the less clutter, the better. Guests will need a place to put their belongings, and even if it's on the floor, having a clean and clear space is a must. If your guest space also doubles as an office, living room, or child's bedroom, take a few minutes to tidy up the space and make room for your guests' belongings before they arrive.

Whether it's an entire room, a sleeper sofa, or an air mattress on the floor, the key to making your guests comfortable is preparing for them ahead of time. A well-thought-out space and plan for their stay will ensure they feel wanted and welcome.

Style ON A BUDGET

If your home and budget don't allow for a designated guest space, invest in a nice air mattress and a memory foam mattress topper. Together, they make an amazingly comfortable bed—it's what we do here at our house for extra guests, and it can be done for under $100. This gives you the comfort of knowing your guests are sleeping well, while still allowing you the flexibility of storing the extra bed elsewhere until it's needed again.

WHERE TO SHOP

AIR MATTRESSES AND MEMORY FOAM TOPPERS
- Amazon
- Target

WELCOME BASKETS AND TRAYS
- Target
- T.J.Maxx

TOWELS AND BLANKETS
- Amazon
- Ross
- Target
- Walmart

@exceeding.joy

Choosing a neutral color for larger items makes a great backdrop for pops of color. This also makes it easy to change out items and refresh the room.

@uncommon.farmhouse

Using items in unexpected ways makes a space feel whimsical.

@tgjghome

Layers and textures give our guest room a comfortable feeling. A pretty coverlet and a folded duvet or comforter across the bed is great for added warmth. Inexpensive, faux-fur throws give a cozy feel.

@uncommon.farmhouse

I love to layer texture and play with décor. It makes a room both inviting and playful.

MAKE YOUR HOUSE A *Home*

CHRISTINE HEBBRING AND JEN MURRAY
www.PaintedFoxHome.com
@paintedfoxhome

Pictured: Christine Hebbring

We are Christine and Jen, a pair of treasure-hunting best friends who are living our dream. We love infusing farmhouse treasures big and small into our lives, and we are so excited to share that passion with you. We truly believe your home should be filled with the people and things you love the most in the world. Our relentless desire to give our own homes a vibe of "farmhouse swag" has inspired us to create Painted Fox Home, our online store specializing in fabulous farmhouse décor.

OUR WHY

We have always been ready for a good hunt—Goodwill, St. Vinny's, Salvation Army, auctions, flea markets, garage sales, art shows, antique malls, estate sales, and even curbside throwaways! We'd always find ourselves wandering in search of the perfect piece, and we began to run out of space. But the trouble was, we hadn't run out of ambition.

Motto for Life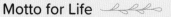

By wisdom a house is built, and by understanding it is established; and by knowledge the rooms are filled with all precious and pleasant riches.
—Proverbs 24:3–4 NASB

That's when we had a lightbulb moment. Why not sell our finds? That way we could share our love of quirky farmhouse objects with a bigger audience. And so Painted Fox Home began.

FAVORITE TIPS

- Fill your home with the people and things you love—*truly love.* Don't let trends define your style. Make it your own, a true reflection of your heart and family.
- Decorate and redecorate your home by shopping your own home first. Sometimes a quick re-arrange can make everything look fresh and new—no spending required!

FIVE MUST-HAVES

1 BED

Obviously, your guests need a bed to sleep on. The size of the bed will depend on the space you have. As I've already mentioned, even an air mattress with a memory foam topper can serve as a comfortable bed for guests. Don't worry so much about the space you have but rather how comfortable your guests will be when they rest their heads.

2 BEDDING

I personally want my guests to sleep better than I do. I want them to have the nicest set of sheets we own and the nicer towels. Consider keeping a set of bedding, blankets, and towels designated just for your guests so they're easy to grab when company comes. Just toss them in the dryer for a few moments with a damp rag and a dryer sheet to freshen them up before guests arrive.

3 LIGHTING

My dad supplies two kinds of light for his guests: a bedside lamp for reading and night-lights for walking to the bathroom and other areas in the dark. As a child, when the night-lights came out, I knew the guests were coming. Make sure your guests have lighting for bedtime reads as well as the middle-of-the-night trip for a glass of water.

4 SPACE

When I have guests come over, I make sure to have areas where they can put their things. For longer stays, I clear out closet areas or drawers. Guests will feel much more settled when their belongings have a place to belong.

5 WELCOME BASKET

Leave your guests a sweet note that welcomes them into their space and provides important information, like the Wi-Fi password. Along with the note, include a basket of essentials they may have forgotten. Providing items like an extra toothbrush, cotton swabs, mouthwash, small shampoos, lotion, bottled water, and snacks will make sure your guests' needs are covered, helping them to relax and focus on having a great time. Fresh flowers and a magazine or two are easy additions that make your guests feel especially welcomed and cared for.

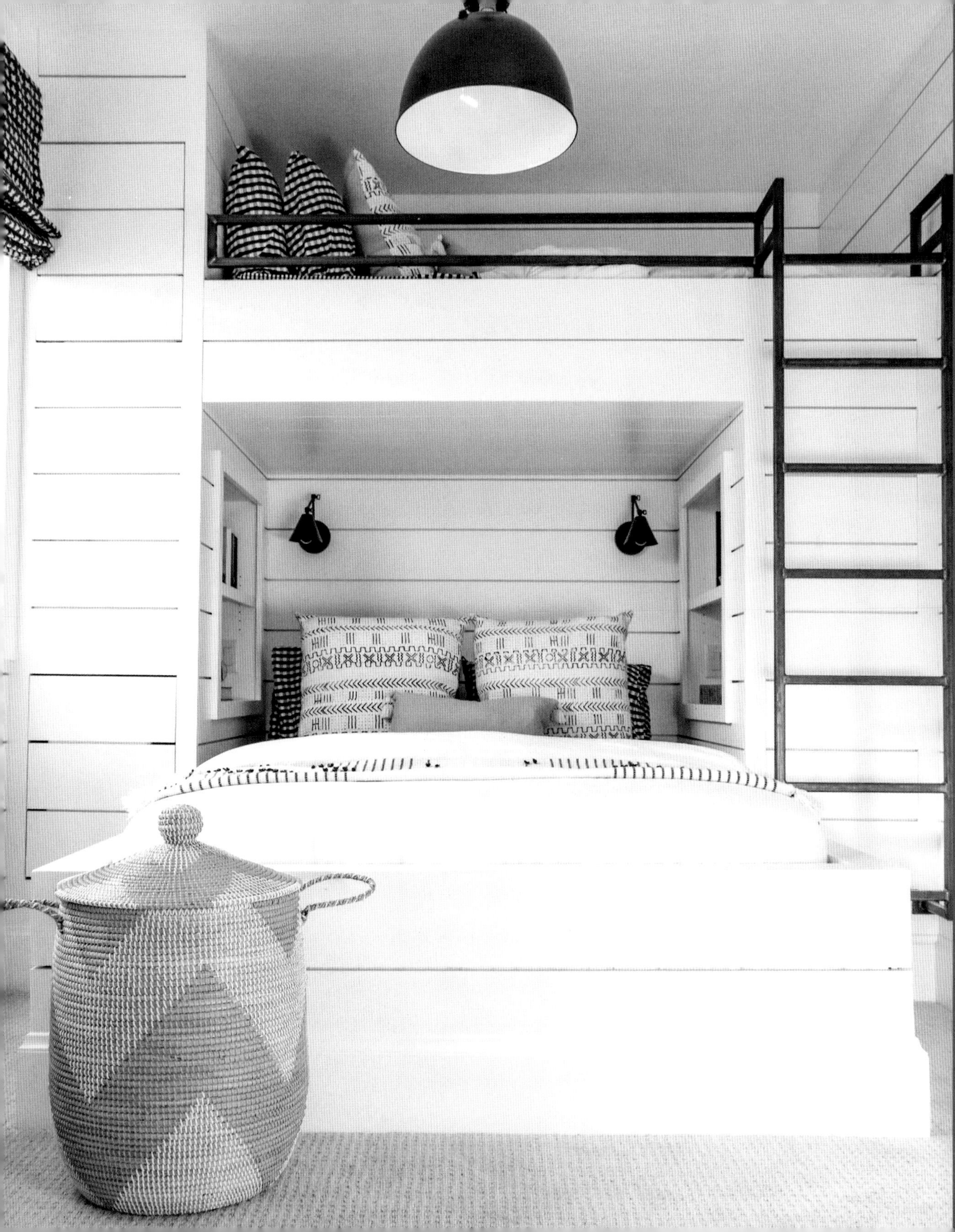

@prettydomesticated

Chapter 8

OUTDOOR SPACES

Nature's peace will flow into you as sunshine flows into trees.

—JOHN MUIR

Why is it when I'm most anxious, I need to step outside? For me, a breath of fresh air—no matter the weather—is always calming. Whether it's the cold, brisk air of winter or that fresh smell after a summer rain, something about the outdoors centers me and allows me to step back into the hustle and bustle with renewed energy. Perhaps being in nature reminds me there is a world out there much bigger than myself and there's One in control of it all. Having a relaxing outside space to release anxiety and restore my focus is imperative for me.

You, yes *you*, can create your own outdoor retreat.

Your outdoor space doesn't have to be a lavish garden, a beautifully screened-in porch,

or a thousand-dollar stone firepit. It can be a simple patio with a couple of chairs, an apartment balcony strung with twinkle lights, or an outdoor bench surrounded by a few potted plants. It's anywhere you can breathe in fresh air and have a quiet moment.

The purpose of an outdoor space is to have an escape from the fast-paced, electronic frenzy of our everyday lives. And creating a space for this, no matter how large or small, will be so rewarding for you and for those you love.

So come with me. Let's step outside and . . . breathe.

LAYOUT AND STYLE

You, yes *you*, can create your own outdoor retreat. Don't get caught up in thinking that a big porch or yard is the only way to make a worthwhile space outside. In fact, the size of the space doesn't matter nearly as much as what you do to it. Our own home has a few different outdoor zones. The front porch features a swing made from our boys' baby crib. Rocking chairs offer the perfect spot for that morning cup of coffee. On our back porch, you'll find a dining area and a small firepit for roasting marshmallows.

If your space is limited, you may not be

able to include a porch swing or firepit. But you probably have more options than you think. First, as always, think about your *why*. What purpose do you want this space to serve?

- Will this area be more kid-oriented or adult-oriented?
- Is it for the whole family, or is it simply for you?
- Do you want to entertain here? If so, how many people will you likely be hosting?
- Do you need a space to eat, to rest, to play, or all of the above?

Next, you'll need to determine what your space can accommodate. If you're limited to a tiny stoop, perhaps you only have room for a pot of flowers or a tiny folding chair. It's still a place to step outside and enjoy nature. If you have a small patio or balcony, a simple bistro set (like this one I use for my she shed; see page 106) invites you and your guest to settle in for coffee and conversation. Add a few hanging plants and some twinkle lights for that little something extra.

For a front porch, rocking chairs, benches, or swings dress up the space and make it feel more welcoming. If your family enjoys

KEEP IT *Tidy*

To stay organized, keep something outside to hold your outdoor items. Outdoor bins are great for storing basketballs and other sports equipment. Pool floats, toys, and other items can be hidden away in totes or outdoor cabinets. On our covered porch, we used an old dining buffet to hold outdoor extras like flashlights and bug spray.

grilling, provide a few Adirondack chairs for gathering around the chef. The plastic ones are inexpensive and easy to spray off and reuse. If you have a large porch or yard, you might want to create an outdoor dining area. We did this on our porch and love eating outside on fall or spring nights. There are plenty of step-by-step plans available online for building your own outdoor tables. Or consider searching OfferUp for older tables you wouldn't mind getting ruined by the elements. Hang a few twinkle lights, and you'll have your own magical outdoor space for entertaining.

A firepit is another way to create an instant gathering place. Portable firepits are inexpensive and easy to find, or create your own with gravel and Adirondack chairs.

What about the kids? Do you want a play area for your kids? What sort of activities would they most enjoy? If you have the space and the budget, put in a swing set or a playhouse. A backyard tree is the perfect place for an old-fashioned tire swing. Because we want our boys to love being outside, we intentionally created spaces they would enjoy.

Shopping for outdoor furniture can be a bit frustrating. There are many options these days, and not all of them are affordable. But you can dress up any space with a colorful outdoor rug, a few twinkle lights, and a pretty umbrella. Take it a step further by adding a few plants, a couple of rocking chairs or Adirondacks, and some outdoor pillows. Use colors that either mimic the outdoors or that flow with the style and colors of your interior design.

Outdoor spaces, no matter how big or small, can give you a sense of peace and separation from the world. They provide a place to enjoy time with friends and family, whether it's sitting around a small firepit or a custom outdoor dining area. So step outside. Take time to breathe deeply, turn off all those devices, and connect with those around you.

Style ON A BUDGET

Twinkle lights can change the feel of an entire space for less than $10 a box. Add your own style with an inexpensive outdoor rug and some outdoor pillows. For those of us who don't have green thumbs, faux plants—especially the ones at IKEA—are an easy, affordable alternative to live greenery.

WHERE TO SHOP

OUTDOOR FURNITURE
- Facebook Marketplace
- Home Depot
- Lowe's
- OfferUp
- VarageSale

OUTDOOR RUGS AND PILLOWS
- Lowe's
- Pier 1
- Target
- Walmart

TWINKLE LIGHTS
- Amazon
- Harbor Freight Tools
- Target

@keely.mann

@simplysoutherncottage

A comfortable outdoor living area to rest and relax is a must, as is a space to gather friends and loved ones. Chains wrapped in rope bring interest and depth to the bed swing and back porch area.

@plankandpillow

Because our house exterior is white, we needed to add some warm wood tones. We achieved this by using wood on the porch ceilings and decking—and, of course, the swing bed.

@plankandpillow

Clean lines were important to us when designing our pool area. We chose a simple rectangular pool surrounded by pavers and grass.

@sanctuaryhomedecor

Find ways to make each season special. On our back porch, piles of fresh and faux pumpkins spill down the steps to celebrate the beginning of fall.

MAKE YOUR HOUSE A *Home*

LESLIE SAETA
www.My100YearOldHome.com
@my100yearoldhome

I never imagined I would become a blogger. But it happened, and it's the best job I have ever had. Growing up I enjoyed crafting, art, creating, and home décor. Now I have a job that includes all of this and more!

My blog titled *My 100 Year Old Home* is all about my home, my lifestyle, and things that can bring joy into life. I love sharing decorating ideas, entertaining tips, crafts, recipes, and ways you can easily make your house a home. As a wife and mother of three boys, I love to entertain. Our home is a gathering place for our family and friends, and nothing makes me happier than sharing what I love to do.

MY WHY

Our home is the greatest gift. It's more than one hundred years old and has so many sto-ries to tell! It's our family's place to gather, and it's loved and worn. The edges of my coffee table are scarred from soccer and baseball cleats—and I love it. Our home is also a bit famous: it has been the setting of more than fifty movies, commercials, and TV shows!

FAVORITE TIPS

- Shop vintage. I am always on the lookout for hidden gems, shopping flea markets, estate sales, and garage sales whenever I can. Yes, most vintage items cost a few dollars more, but I love giving these special pieces a new home.

- Keep it neutral. Decorating is so much easier when you start with a neutral color palette. When it comes to investment pieces of furniture, buy them in neutral colors. If you already have a dark or patterned sofa,

Motto for Life

Write it on your heart that every
day is the best day in the year.

—Ralph Waldo Emerson

have a slipcover made in a lighter color. Add
color and patterns with art, accessories, bedding, slipcovers, and rugs.

@sanctuaryhomedecor

Outdoor dining areas can make meals and conversations especially memorable. The porch on our Montana ranch is a popular gathering place for our friends and family to enjoy a good meal and time together.

@thegingerhome

A screen room can extend the outdoor living season and is a versatile and multifunctional space. It offers shade and mosquito-free dining in the summer and a cozy spot to curl up by the fire in the spring and fall! We use our screen room addition as a family room, dining space, and party venue. We even use it as a yoga pavilion! Don't be afraid to think outside the box and make your spaces work for you in multiple ways.

FIVE MUST-HAVES

1 SEATING

Somewhere to plop down, relax, and unwind outside is essential. It can be simple, like fold-out chairs for two, or elaborate, like a dining area and firepit.

2 A TABLE OR TWO

It's always nice to have a table for holding drinks, books, or magazines. Depending on the size of your space, it might be a small side table, an outdoor coffee table, or even a full-size dining table.

3 LIGHTS

We use tiki torches around our porch. Not only do they keep pesky bugs away, but they also illuminate the space at night (all for a great price!). And hanging outdoor twinkle lights makes any space magical.

4 PILLOWS

Outdoor pillows are fabulous! Not only can they get wet, but they can also stand up to being outdoors all season long—and they make your outdoor seating much more comfortable and inviting.

@beautifulchaos.home

5 PLANTS

Plants add so much style and warmth to your outdoor space. Change them up seasonally or for the holidays. If you don't have a green thumb, add a faux cactus or a faux fiddle leaf fig tree or two. Try pairing them with planters filled with seasonal flowers.

There is nothing like staying at home for real comfort.

—JANE AUSTEN

People often ask how I maintain an organized and clean home. Let's be honest: it's not always clean or organized. There are days when dishes sit in the sink and dirty laundry doesn't make it to the washer. But I do have a decent system that keeps my home flowing smoothly, even on the busiest days.

The foundation of this system—and the best advice I have—is to give all your things a designated "home" to return to. This is so important! My kids have areas for their toys, and I have areas for my bills. Socks go in one bucket and shoes in another. We have loose change jars near the key basket and in our master bedroom closet because emptying pockets seems to happen in those two areas.

My point is this: if we train ourselves to put certain things in certain places, we create a habit of staying organized. Then, no matter what we're doing—whether it's speeding through the morning routine to get out the door, preparing for that video conference in the home office, or having a playdate with the kids on the living room floor—those designated spaces

Give all your things a designated "home" to return to.

for our things will ensure we leave no (or at least fewer) traces of clutter behind.

Take some time to evaluate where your struggle zones are. Is it the mound of shoes by the back door? Get something as simple as a large tote bucket and place it by the door. Is it the excessive amount of clothes in your closet? Try getting rid of things that are threadbare or don't fit with your style anymore (or those

pesky pants that you're hoping to squeeze into again one day). It's time to purge. It's time to evaluate where your organization is lacking and tackle those trouble spots head-on.

In my experience, the most troublesome zones are the office space (for the pesky paperwork and bills); kids' rooms (for the excessive toys); mudrooms, laundry rooms, and closets (for all those piles of often-random stuff); and pantries (where unused ingredients go to expire).

Let's tackle some organization together, shall we?

@thegingerhome

Chapter 9

OFFICE

*Everyone needs a space to work,
a space to dream, a space to become
who they were meant to be.*

In all the homes I can remember, even from childhood, we've had an office space. My mother occasionally worked from home when I was young, and now my husband and I do. And because our children are homeschooled, they're always doing their work at home too. We each need a designated space to work.

The office can be a space of your own to dream, work, and create.

In our first home, once the baby came, the office become a nursery. My husband would work from the kitchen table, papers spread all over. I remember him saying, "One day I want my own space to retreat to." I think that's important—to have an "office" to retreat to. It doesn't have to be an entire room set aside just for you, but it can be a space of your own to dream, work, and create. Life revolves so much around work. So designating a space for that work can not only help you stay organized but also help you end your workday when you want to be present elsewhere.

We were blessed to be able to incorporate a home office into our current home. I designed it to be a more masculine retreat for my husband. He uses it daily. It's *his* space. I've seen him smile and sigh with confidence and contentment when he sits down at his desk. It's amazing how a space can encourage both of those feelings. My own office tends to be wherever I'm needed most at the moment, but I do have a spot carved out in my laundry room for all my paperwork and projects to "belong." I have a built-in desk that houses my computer, current reads, and those ever-present bills. It gives me a place to take the mail and sort through my daily to-do list. Although my "office" is also home to the laundry and the boys' schoolwork, it is still my zone. Having a space to call your own—a place to gather and regroup—is just so important.

Think about the areas in your home. Where can you create an office-like setting? Do you have room for a corner desk, or do you have an entire room to use for an office? Where can you sit to dream, write, pay bills, or scroll through your favorite blogs? And while the purpose of an office is to have a place to work, you'll find that having a space to work in that you're proud of will fill you with feelings of confidence and contentment too.

So let's get to work on your office space.

LAYOUT AND STYLE

Before working on the layout of your office space, decide who will be using it and what

KEEP IT *Tidy*

Create a drop zone for your daily mail. I have a basket by my desk for incoming and outgoing mail. I check it about once a week to keep tabs on what's coming and going. I also have an "office in a basket" (just as I do for my kids' home-schooling things). It contains my planner, pens, stamps, folders categorizing my bills and current work items, binder clips, and envelopes—everything I need to pay bills and plan ahead, as well any current projects I'm working on. I can get it out all at once, spread it across the dining room table, and then easily put it away again when I'm finished. I also like to keep my planner on the desk where I can easily see my daily to-do tasks. All my appointments and events go into my Google calendar—it's an easy way to share them with my husband, and it helps us keep up with each other!

they will be using it for. Ask yourself these questions:

- Do you need space to pay bills and meet deadlines?
- Do you or your spouse work from home? Do you need a separate home office?
- Do your kids need a designated space for homework?
- How large of a space do you need?

@lovecarriej

Once you've answered these questions, you can begin to work on the layout. The focal point of any office is a desk, tabletop, or writing space—somewhere to take your thoughts and somewhere to leave them. If you don't have a designated room to use for an office, you can create a small office "zone" just about anywhere. Hang a few floating shelves above a desk and anchor the area with a rug. Be creative! Turn a guest room closet into a built-in desk area. Hang a dream board, artwork, or prints of favorite verses or quotes to reflect who is using the space. By using the same style furniture you've used in the rest of the house, you'll create cohesiveness. For example, my husband wanted a more masculine office. I used a few antique items on the walls to stay in tune with the rest of the house, but then we agreed to a modern cowhide rug to appease his desire for masculinity. Even if your office is simply the corner of another room, by using elements similar to those used in the rest of the house, your office space will feel like it's part of the overall intentional design.

An office is more than just a place to get your work done. It's where you dive into your dreams, finish up those daily tasks, and gather yourself. Whether you have a desk against a wall or an entire room dedicated to your work, create a space for you (or someone else in your family) to be productive, imagine, and dream.

Style ON A BUDGET

You may feel pressured to invest in a desk, but there are many inexpensive options out there, especially if you aren't looking for a traditional-style desk. Or if you like to tackle DIY projects, make your own! Try topping two filing cabinets or small bookcases with a wooden door. Or attach a wooden board to two flat-topped wooden barstools. You don't have to break the bank when you're willing to get creative! And when it comes to your office chair, make sure it not only blends with your style but is comfortable too. Add the perfect lamp for lighting, and you'll be ready for business.

WHERE TO SHOP

DESKS
- Amazon
- Facebook Marketplace
- OfferUp
- Office Depot
- Wayfair

OFFICE CHAIRS
- Pier 1
- Wayfair
- World Market

OFFICE AND DESK LIGHTING
- Hobby Lobby
- Target
- T.J.Maxx
- Walmart

@plankandpillow

Since we work from home, having a space that helps us focus and be creative is important to us. We designed this room to be light, airy, and modern. Then we added a focal point in the form of a dark, vertical shiplap accent wall.

@prettydomesticated

Drama isn't always complicated. A bright art piece paired with dark walls and an IKEA hack built-in create a straightforward and one-of-a-kind look. Don't be afraid to take risks. It's half the fun!

@themorrismanor

If you can't add beams or a coffered ceiling, a chandelier is a great way to create interest.

@simplysoutherncottage

An office should exude calm and simplicity. I created a beautiful work environment with a neutral color palette to help focus my attention while working in this space.

MAKE YOUR HOUSE A *Home*

MELONIE GRAVES
www.TheMellionaireHouse.com
@themellionairehouse

I am the creator of The Mellionaire House, a home décor and lifestyle brand located in Tampa, Florida. A third-generation Tampa native, I have a passion for living a full and abundant life. I am a wife, a mother to three amazing children (including *twins!*), and a dream chaser. After a successful seventeen-year career in advertising and marketing, I left corporate America to spend more time with my family and to pursue happiness.

I have created a lifestyle brand dedicated to contributing content that will inspire people, especially women, in some way. Through social platforms, I share the daily lives of my family, along with information on parenting, home décor trends, DIY tips,

holiday styling (my personal favorite), meal ideas, wine and cocktails, and much more!

MY WHY
I believe there truly is no place like home. Your home should be a place of peace and a reflection of who you are—which means I tend to make my own rules when it comes to design and décor. Because I want our home to feel warm and inviting, I often style our spaces with warm metals and neutral tones.

FAVORITE TIPS
- Make your bed every single day.
- Don't forget to check places like Habitat for Humanity ReStore—and check often!

Their stock is always changing. You'll find anything from brand-new light fixtures to cabinets and small appliances, all at very affordable prices!

- Add cleaning vinegar, which is more acidic than regular white vinegar, to the rinse cycle of your laundry for extra fresh and fluffy towels!

FIVE MUST-HAVES

1 A DESK

The desk can be as traditional or as creative as you want. Really, you just need a flat, workable space. It can be a drop-down desk that attaches to the wall and folds down for access, a small table tucked into a converted closet, or an old makeup vanity. I found my husband's desk on Amazon for a very affordable price. With its industrial style, it fits his more rustic vibe. A sleek metal desk may appeal to your modern-leaning tastes, or perhaps it's an antique secretary that speaks to your vintage-loving heart. Think about your own personal style and find the desk that best suits you.

2 A CHAIR

Every desk needs a chair. And if you're going to be working, you might as well be comfortable. Design and style may be more important to me than most, but comfort should take priority in your chair choice, especially if you'll sit there a lot. I prefer upholstered chairs, and my husband likes the look of leather. Both are great options! And don't worry—office chairs aren't all black and fake plastic anymore. The options are endless, so find one that fits your style and needs.

3 A RUG

Aren't you surprised I'm recommending a rug? But a rug *really does* define a space, especially if your office is part of another room. Putting one under your desk and chair will instantly give your space the "feel" of an office. My husband chose cowhide for his office, giving the whole room a more masculine feel.

4 LAMPS

Working in bright overhead light can strain your eyes. Tone down the lighting and warm up the atmosphere with a lamp or two. This may mean a floor lamp, traditional desk lamp, or wall-mounted lighting. Better yet, try a battery-operated lightbulb. Gone are the days of wiring an electrical fixture. You can now attach *any* wall sconce or light fixture to the wall and simply add a battery-operated lightbulb.

5 ORGANIZATION AND STORAGE

Use baskets, stackable storage, or filing cabinets to hide items you don't want to see. I like to keep a basket on my desk to hold bills and other items that need attention. A desk calendar, drawer organizers, and a cup for pens and pencils are a few ways to keep your desktop clean and organized.

@finding_lovely

Chapter 10

KIDS' ROOMS AND SPACES

The laughter of a child is the light of the home.

My mom used to let my sister and me recreate our spaces every year or two, and that meant the world to me! I knew my wishes were considered and my opinions mattered. Even if my room didn't match my mom's taste at all, she let my space grow up with me and reflect who I was. Looking back, I realize the opportunity to craft my own room pushed me toward design. That freedom to explore my own style gave me confidence and a passion for what I do. Moms, you may never know the impact such an opportunity can have on your child. So thank you, Mom!

Giving kids independence in their spaces helps their confidence grow.

Just like adults, it's equally important for kids to have some part of the home—a room or a corner—that reflects who they are, an area where their creativity and individuality can be showcased. I have two boys, and while they aren't necessarily into home design, they still have opinions about what they do and don't like. For example, when we picked quilts for their rooms, they chose blue quilts over green ones. And when we shopped for art, my oldest approved the word art and told me which animals he preferred. Even littles have big opinions, and I think it's important to hear and honor their requests—at least the reasonable ones!

As you style your kids' spaces, don't forget that they will grow (so quickly!) and their tastes will change. So, yes, design that adorable nursery, but as you make your style

choices, keep an eye to the future and how you can adjust for the toddler to teen years.

While my children have their own rooms, as well as a playroom, they always seem to end up wherever we are. And honestly, I love that. I know this may change as they get older, so I try to treasure these times together. Even though I enjoy having them with us, my kids do have zones for their stuff. By creating zones for them, I'm able to give my sons their own areas while keeping a sense of order and a bit of sanity.

So grab your kids, and let's create their space.

LAYOUT AND STYLE

Whether it's the bedrooms, a playroom, or a designated kids' zone, first decide on the purpose that particular area needs to serve.

- Will the child or children do more than sleep here?
- Will you need this room to also serve as a play or study area?

The needs you have will determine your layout. I recommend two zones: one for sleeping and one for playing, studying, or reading. As you design your kids' space, focus on creating a place for them to lay their heads and also a corner for books or a tent for make-believe. If you have teens or tweens, consider giving them a work space for homework and a computer. If space allows, upgrade them to a larger bed to accommodate their growing stature. I still remember going from a twin bed to a full-size bed and thinking my whole world had changed!

Do you need bunk beds to house your children? These days, there are some stylish bunk beds, and many offer built-in storage options. Be sure to choose furniture that will grow with your child. Many cribs convert into toddler beds and then to full-size beds, so as your child grows, you'll need to replace the mattress but not the whole bed. And remember, even though that race car or princess bed looks fun now, you will end up replacing it before you can blink. A simple bed with easily changed race car or princess bedding will make everyone happy.

Next, think about storage. Does your child need a dresser, a bookshelf, a desk, or a place for toys? If you are low on closet space, consider a wardrobe to store extra items. Keep furniture simple and neutral to accommodate changing tastes as children grow older. Before

investing in larger storage pieces, consider what their future storage needs will be. Your baby boy's clothes might not take up much room now, but that will be a completely different story when he's sixteen.

- Keep in mind that themed rooms, while cute, don't age with the child. So if you are looking for a long-term investment, try sticking to neutral design decisions and adding fun accents that reflect the child's age. For my kids' rooms, I keep the walls and furniture neutral and dress up other areas with color.

For example, my oldest son has a dark gray bunk bed, and we play with colors in the rug and patterns in his bedspreads. In my youngest son's black and white room, we bring color in with other fun elements like my dad's antique red fire truck. You can even create an accent wall in a kid's space using stencils, wallpaper, or board-and-batten. For my youngest son's room, I added a DIY stencil for under $5. The Swiss cross transformed the room and

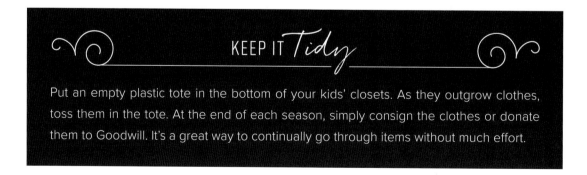

KEEP IT *Tidy*

Put an empty plastic tote in the bottom of your kids' closets. As they outgrow clothes, toss them in the tote. At the end of each season, simply consign the clothes or donate them to Goodwill. It's a great way to continually go through items without much effort.

added something visually pleasing for an affordable price. Look what my friend Carrie (@lovecarriej) did in her children's rooms with simple accents walls. Amazing!

- As your kids grow, allow their rooms to grow with them. Try changing the lighting or hanging a fun chandelier. Switch their themed art and bedding for styles more suited to their maturing tastes. Try to give older kids a space to dream, draw, and study. Change those kid-friendly zones you've had scattered around the house into areas more tailored to the interests of an older child.

- Be sure to ask for their opinions. Trust me, if your teens are anything like I was growing up, they'll have even more of an opinion than ever before. It's important to still listen and honor their opinions, helping them to create a sanctuary they can retreat to. I've found older kids like simplicity in design. They aren't looking for the

@lovecarriej

fluff and frill of childhood but want to transition into a more minimalist adult area that includes a work space.

Too often children get left out of the design equation. But their little minds are ready to be a part of the home you create just as much as any other member of the family. Giving kids independence in their spaces helps their confidence grow. So don't forget the kiddos when you're designing their spaces.

Style ON A BUDGET

Buy quilts for kids' beds. I'm not talking about a quilt like the one your grandmother sewed by hand but rather a fun patterned or floral quilt. My oldest has a plaid quilt in blue that I either fold on the end of his bed for added color or use across the bed. Quilts allows kids to express their own style without breaking the bank. And I have found that quilts are more durable, lasting longer than the average comforter. Because they aren't as bulky, they're also much easier to wash. To further personalize the space, get crafty with cutouts and decals. Hang twinkle lights for an inexpensive way to create a magical space.

WHERE TO SHOP		
KIDS' ROOM FURNITURE	**QUILTS**	**KIDS' DÉCOR**
• IKEA	• Amazon	• Hobby Lobby
• Target	• Target	
	• T.J.Maxx	

@lovecarriej

My oldest son loves architecture and streamlined designs, so for his room we used clean lines and contrast, mixed with some rich wood tones. He picked the gray hue and couldn't be more pleased with it.

@jesswasserman

We long for our house to have an unmistakable feeling of *home*. We've put a lot of thought into getting décor just right, and it brings me so much joy to fill every nook and cranny with special little memories and love. In the playroom I sprinkled twinkle lights, old books from my childhood, and lots of comfy pillows and rugs to make playtime extra cozy.

@oldsaltfarm

To bring light to the space and to maintain ceiling height, we kept the basement ceiling unfinished and then painted everything white. We also built a large closet with barn doors for toys and games. It's the perfect space to play!

@ourvictorianitaliante

The kids' area should be a space they want to be in. Display their artwork and make it easy for them to maintain. Use oversize storage containers for crayons and markers, and use buckets or baskets that keep papers in one place.

MAKE YOUR HOUSE A *Home*

ERIN KERN

www.CottonStem.com
@cottonstem

'm an Oklahoma mom of four girls, chasing dreams while chasing babies. I'm all about home design, style, and motherhood—plus a little "cray" along the way! My blog, *Cotton Stem*, is a way to bring a light to my social media community while serving and inspiring along the way.

MY WHY

My daughters are my four tiny reasons for making our house into a home. They're the four reasons I give grace to others and to myself. (The latter is sometimes hardest, isn't it?) They're why I am who I am, why I pray harder, smile bigger, and hope to heaven I'm doing this whole mommin' gig the best that I can. In other words, they're the sweetest little "whys" I know.

FAVORITE TIPS

- Stay true to your own sense of what is beautiful, no matter what others around you are doing.
- Make your home a place where your people feel like they can actually *live*, not simply tiptoe around the beautiful décor.
- Don't be afraid of a few holes in the wall! Dare to create!

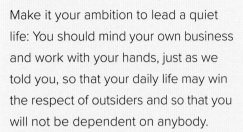

Motto for Life

Make it your ambition to lead a quiet life: You should mind your own business and work with your hands, just as we told you, so that your daily life may win the respect of outsiders and so that you will not be dependent on anybody.

—1 Thessalonians 4:11–12 NIV

1 FUN DÉCOR

Your kids' décor doesn't have to match the rest of your home, but their spaces can reflect their interests without having cartoons all over your walls. For boys, I go with plaid or checks for the bedspread, then let them have that Spider-Man pillow. If your little girl loves mermaids, get her mermaid sheets that coordinate with a more neutral quilt on top. There are also peel-and-stick wallpapers and decals that easily transform a drab wall into something eye-catching. The cartoons and themes don't have to take over the room. Stay neutral and accent with accessories.

2 SOMETHING EXTRA PLAYFUL

Provide something playful in your kids' rooms or spaces. My kids have a small barn door that leads into a finished-out attic space. The door slides open to reveal a hidden play space. But you don't have to have a built-in area for play. Kids love being "in" and "under," so a place for a fabric teepee or fort in the corner makes a great little hideaway for big imaginations. I've even seen swings and faux rock walls in older kids' spaces. Set up a tent or small reading nook with pillows and twinkle lights. Put up fun decals or wallpaper

to give them an imaginative space. We also hung lights from the boys' bedside walls, and they love turning them on and off because they each have one. Small, fun ideas go a long way with kids.

3 ZONES

We make slime, play outside, and get dirty, but the kids know their zones and where the creative messes are allowed. These zones are the key to keeping your kids' stuff tidy, and you should have them in a few different spaces within your home. This allows your kids to still be with you in a space, while keeping their stuff from taking over. Where do your kids create their art, put together puzzles, or play with LEGOs? Create a zone for those activities with baskets for stashing stuff when it's not in use. Designate a shelf on your bookcase for their books. Set up an "office" zone for homework. Because we homeschool, each child has his own basket with his curriculum inside. This approach will work with any child, homeschooled or not. Have a basket for each child to hold favorite books, coloring pages, or games. Kids can easily pull them out and put them away again.

My boys have areas for toys downstairs and upstairs. They are hidden as much as possible in baskets or built-ins with doors. Their toys are organized so that their puzzles are all together and easily reachable. LEGOs are in their own bin for easy access. A hutch holds games and art supplies. These zones around the house keep items contained but also give the kids areas all throughout the house for play. For older kids and teenagers, you may need space to corral card games and video games. Of course, the size of the home determines how much space you have for kids' play and work areas, but having zones

@cottonstem

in another. Action figures, dolls, art supplies, books—each gets assigned its own tote, bin, or shelf. If your items have homes, I promise it's easier to keep up with the mess. Kids catch on too. My oldest takes pride in his things (especially because he doesn't want his younger brother destroying them), so more often than not, his toys get put back where they came from.

5 GIVEAWAY BIN

In addition to keeping a bin in the kids' closets for outgrown clothes, I also keep a bin for toys and games they no longer use. My boys help decide what goes in here. We talk about what to give away to kids in need and what to sell to make room for new things. Grab your own bin and stash it in a closet or the garage. Simply drop in items as you come across them—and perhaps do a focused roundup two or three times a year. By putting everything in a bin, they'll be ready to take to charity or to the next consignment sale.

for toys and activities keeps them busy in different areas of the home—and lets them know that it's their home too.

4 TOTES AND STORAGE BINS

Organize! Use clear storage bins to separate and categorize toys so kids can clearly see them. Put stuffed animals in one tote, puzzles

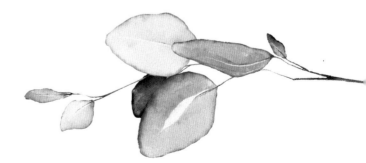

Laundry Co.

WASH . DRY AND FOLD

EST. 1952

Chapter 11

MUDROOM, LAUNDRY ROOM, AND CLOSETS

Sometimes you just have to bless the mess.

There are some places in the home that seem to create their own kind of chaos. And you probably know the places I'm talking about: the mudroom, laundry room, and closets—pretty much *every* closet. These are spaces that definitely need grace. But by creating some form of organization in these areas of your home, you may not lose your sanity.

You just need somewhere to catch the chaos!

In our current home we are blessed to have a mudroom. It's designed to house things we need to access easily but don't want strewn inside the house. In our first home, we didn't have a mudroom, so I created a sort of mini-mudroom near the door with hooks for jackets and a cabinet for shoes. Whether you have a whole room or just a wall by the door, you can create a more organized space for all your gear.

The laundry room is another area, at least in my home, that becomes the landing place of random things. A loose earring, a few pairs of shoes, the basket of mismatched socks, and things that get shoved there in a rush when company is coming over. You know I'm right! Yes, the laundry room is one of those chaotic zones. Even now, my laundry room houses both my office and craft table—you can imagine all the stuff in this room. All those odds and ends can be overwhelming, and just walking inside can be stressful.

I expect many of you may feel the same way about your laundry rooms. As with other spaces, it all comes down to creating zones and organization, and that's the only thing that helps me control the chaos—at least some of the time.

And then there are the closets. Growing up, our closets at home were always tidy, thanks to my dad. My mom tended to keep the house tidy and clean, but her closet? That was another story! (Sorry, Mom.) Dad kept his side immaculate, while Mom's was just like her personality—and let's just say she's the fun one.

My sister took after my mom, and, well, I got my dad's knack for organization. Matching hangers all pointed in the same direction, perfectly lined-up shoes and accessories arranged in neat little rows—these are the things that make my heart happy. I know everyone isn't stricken with the tidiness disease, but I will tell you, it helps immensely when you're trying to get dressed or searching for a particular toy. Yes, closets are a challenge, but getting rid of clutter and creating organization is the key to calming that closet chaos.

Come on, let's start clearing away and creating calm.

LAYOUT AND STYLE

Mudroom

If you have a mudroom, that's where to corral your "coming and going" gear. If you don't have a mudroom, evaluate where you and your family drop your larger gear most frequently. Next, think about the items you need to organize.

- Are there shoes lying around?
- Do you want easy access to coats, bags, or backpacks?
- Should sports gear have a spot?
- Do you need an area for socks, hats, and mittens?

You can make a mini-mudroom in a hallway for your family's regularly dropped items. Add hooks to a wall for holding coats, bags, and backpacks. Hang matching canvas bags to hold smaller items like mittens and hats. If you have room, place a narrow bench along

Style ON A BUDGET

Organization is the key to calming chaos in these spaces. Just a few containers, baskets, and bins can tidy the clutter. To make clothes sorting easier, pick up an extra laundry basket or two. For the most amazing collection of hooks I've seen, check out Hobby Lobby. You'll be sure to find something that fits your style.

WHERE TO SHOP

BINS AND STORAGE CONTAINERS
- Amazon
- Dollar Tree
- Target

HOOKS AND HANGING STORAGE
- Hobby Lobby
- Home Depot
- Lowe's

the wall and stash bins or baskets underneath to catch shoes and socks. To cut down the clutter, store only the most frequently worn shoes here. Even transforming a small coat closet into a mini-mudroom is a great way to use space you already have. You just need somewhere to catch the chaos!

Laundry Room

As you set up the laundry area, be sure to incorporate a flat area for folding clothes, along with a rod or hooks to hang clothes. I've seen hooks on walls and vintage racks for those "hang to dry" items.

You'll also want a few baskets for sorting clothes. I like to sort my clothes when they come out of the dryer according to the room they belong in. So I have an upstairs basket, a master closet basket, and a towel basket. As I'm pulling items from the dryer, I simply place them in their designated basket, which makes putting laundry away much easier. A beautiful rolling laundry basket can make you feel a little better about that pile of clothes to put away.

If you don't have cabinets in your laundry area, store detergents and other items

in a basket or container, or transfer them to pretty glass jars. Make simple changes that add beauty or warmth to the space. My laundry room has a fun vintage chandelier over the washer and dryer and floral wallpaper on the back wall. Why? If I can make doing laundry more enjoyable by making the space aesthetically appealing, then I definitely will. It feels less like a chore when your space makes you happy.

Closets

My best tip for closets is to declutter as much as possible. Donate clothes that you haven't worn in years to someone who will be thrilled to have them. Get rid of toys your kids aren't playing with. Create a "memorabilia bin" for each family member to hold keepsakes. Store wrapping paper, gift bags, and tissue together in one place.

I've said it before, but I can't say it enough: give your items a home, and it will be so much easier to return them to it. If you have plenty of closets, designate one for cleaning supplies, another for coats, one for linens, and another for games. If you are lacking in the storage department (and who isn't?), try creating zones within the closets you do have for those same items. Also consider other, inconspicuous ways to store items. Benches with storage underneath and rolling bins tucked under couches and inside hutches are useful places to store items out of sight.

These areas—the mudroom, laundry room, and closets—can either be organized or drive you crazy. They're the spaces that need grace in every home. Take some time to organize and create systems that work for you.

MAKE YOUR HOUSE A *Home*

ALLISON AARS

www.TheFestiveFarmhouse.com
@thefestivefarmhouse

'm a Texas girl, born and raised, and self-taught in the school of design. I love to write, create, and encourage every soul I meet. I believe three things: everything starts with the heart, the key to life is gratitude, and every day should be celebrated. That's why I created *The Festive Farmhouse*, an online blog and shop that provides meaningful gifts made easy. It's the perfect niche for my creative-seeking, heart-talk-loving, gift-giving soul. I love to connect with others through life's biggest moments, to give them words when they have none,

and to brighten the darkest of days with gifts straight from the heart.

As a family, we preach the importance of following your bliss. We believe God's plan for us begins when we surrender ours, tune into the unique gifts He's given us, and share them with the world. That's when we truly shine.

MY WHY

My why? *Me.* I know, I know, it's not the usual answer of "my family" or "my kids," and it may even sound selfish—but it's the truth.

Motto for Life
Follow your bliss!

Years ago, I learned the hard way that the only way to fail is to put yourself last. I started my shop at a low point in my life so I could become myself again. I was lost, so I turned to my gifts. I *created* in order to restore my soul. And slowly but surely, one day at a time, I became who God intended me to be all along.

FAVORITE TIPS

- Trust your instinct. Because above all, what you are creating is *yours*. Get feedback, ask for advice, but at the end of the day, choose what makes *your* heart happy.

- Don't aim for perfection. First of all, perfection is a myth—let's just start with that. Second, it's highly overrated. Remember, you're making a home, not a museum. A home should be filled with love, laundry, and mismatched lamps. It should reflect your family's personality, needs, and hopes for the future. Make it real. Make it livable. And you will have made yourself a *home*.

- Gratitude. That may not seem like it has anything to do with home décor, but trust me, it does. When it comes to the world of design, it's easy to always want more. In reality, making a home begins with loving what you *have*. Paint your walls with gratitude, and you will always love the space you live in.

@white.farmhouse

Let's face it. We spend a lot of time doing laundry, and if you like to line-dry your clothes like I do, easy access to a clothesline is a must-have. During the cold Canadian winters, I use the ladder for hanging our clothes. It saves energy, and your clothes will last longer too!

@farmhousechic4sure

A home should have character and functionality, and it should reflect who you are. Adding design elements like built-in lockers and baskets accomplishes just that while creating a one-of-a-kind look.

@bigfamilylittlefarmhouse

Laundry is no fun, but it can be more bearable when you add a little shiplap or wallpaper to your space. Think light and bright! Add some plants (real or faux) for a pop of color, and a big sign as a focal point.

@plankandpillow

I love the built-in lockers my husband, Henry, created for our laundry room—in fact, they're my favorite part! They're a great place for the kids to drop backpacks and shoes as they come in from school.

MAKE YOUR HOUSE A *Home*

TONI HAMMERSLEY

www.ABowlFullofLemons.net
@abowlfulloflemons

I am the woman behind *A Bowl Full of Lemons*, a blog I have been writing since 2010 about homekeeping, home organization, cleaning, French farmhouse–style decorating, budgeting, and healthy living. You may also know me from my bestselling books, *The Complete Book of Home Organization* and *The Complete Book of Clean*. I'm also a registered nurse, a photographer, a wife of twenty-two years, and a mother of three. Beautiful Charleston, South Carolina, is our home.

MY WHY

I strive for a simplified and clutter-free home. It allows me to see what matters most more clearly. By removing the things we no longer have any use for, we are making room for the things that bring us the greatest happiness.

FAVORITE TIPS

- If you don't love it, use it, or need it, let it go.
- For every new purchase you bring into your home, donate an item to make room for it.

Motto for Life

I can do all things through Christ who strengthens me.
—Philippians 4:13 NKJV

FIVE MUST-HAVES

1 HOOKS

Hooks are one of the easiest and most affordable ways to organize household items, from jackets to bags to umbrellas. Take a small portion of a wall and hang about two to five hooks, depending on your needs. Give each child his or her own hook. Place them low so kids can reach them. I use hooks in my hallway, in my mudroom, in the bathroom for towels, in the laundry room for those delicates that need to hang-dry, and even to hold brooms and mops. Trust me: hooks work!

2 BASKETS

I keep baskets all over my house, especially for shoes. Whether you have one huge basket or several smaller ones, baskets cull the clutter! I keep socks in one and shoes in another, right by the back door. That way, I'm not rushing upstairs for socks and back down again for shoes. Everything is in one place. On occasion, my kids will even put their shoes back in the basket. Use baskets in your laundry room for storing laundry necessities like detergent, bleach, and dryer sheets. Baskets in closets can store practically anything, from hats and mittens to T-shirts and toys.

3 BENCHES

If you have room for a bench, it's a great way to create the look of an actual mudroom. Put the bench against the wall, and add baskets underneath—or, better yet, find a bench that doubles as storage. Hang your hooks above the bench, and you've created a mini-mudroom!

4 DÉCOR

Practical areas can also be pretty. Hang a mirror above your bench or beside your row of hooks. Add a fun and inspiring wall quote in the laundry room. Paint the inside of your closets with a pop of color or add pretty shelf paper.

5 AN OUTDOOR RUG

It may seem odd to use an outdoor rug in your mudroom or laundry room, but it will withstand the traffic of wet and dirty shoes. A rug will also add a pop of style and remain easy to clean.

@simplysoutherncottage

SUPER MARK

Mom's BAKING
Fresh Daily Delicious
BREAD·BISCUITS

Light bulbs

pasta

rice

SUGAR

POPCORN

CHOCOLATE

POWDERED SUGAR

FLOUR

tea

Lanter

FARM sweet FARM

1
2 3
4 5 6
7 8 9
10
11 12 13 14
15 16 17 18 19
20

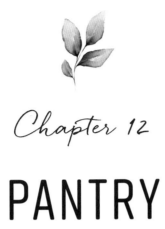

Chapter 12

PANTRY

*Eat your food with joy, and drink your wine with
a happy heart, for God approves of this!*

—ECCLESIASTES 9:7 NLT

The pantry looks different for all of us. It may be a few small cabinets or a large and airy closet. Whatever the size, it's the dreaded space we put off cleaning. (One time, I think found candy sprinkles from my childhood. Just kidding!) We all need grace in the pantry.

We all need grace in the pantry.

I can't believe I'm admitting this, but as a child, I took it upon myself to organize the pantry. I was fed up with the piles of cereal boxes, random cans, and bags. In reality, it probably wasn't that bad, but I still remember beaming with pride after organizing that pantry, knowing my parents would be thrilled with the outcome. Yes, firstborn overachiever here!

When we moved into our current home, I knew I wanted our pantry space to be clean and organized. Baskets and containers helped me achieve that. As we make Saturday morning pancakes, I tell them, "Bottom basket for the flour, boys!" And after they get home from school a little peckish, I can say, "Snacks are in the snack bin on the third shelf," a place where they can reach them. Cereals are in clear dispensers on the counter, making it easy to see what needs to be refilled. But my biggest tip for the pantry is to first get in there and clean it out!

So come on, take a deep breath, and let's dive into that pantry together.

LAYOUT AND STYLE

As you think about the layout of your pantry, consider these questions:

- What space do you have to work with?
- What foods do you consume the most?
- How can they be organized a little better for your needs?

The next step is to pull out all the food and organize it by category. Baking goes in one pile, cereal and breakfast food in another, and so on. These piles will tell you how many baskets you need. Get items off the floor and consider adding hanging storage organizers to your pantry or cabinet doors. I can't say it enough: a pantry can be clean and organized *if and only if* items have a home and everyone knows where to put them.

Remember, organization can be pretty too. Look for baskets that complement tones in the rest of your house. Choose containers that match your overall design choices. Glass jars are an attractive way to store flour, sugar, and cornmeal. Choose something sleek and simple for a modern home, classic white for traditional, jewel tones for an eclectic style, and chipped enamel or vintage jars for a more rustic look. Having clear containers helps you

Every so often, we need to purge the pantry by clearing it out and organizing it anew. But in between those purges, try this trick: whenever you bring in new groceries, throw out the old things you no longer need, dump the crumbs from the chip basket, and toss any stale or expired items—along with potatoes that have started growing eyes. Do this each time you put groceries away, and it will keep the pantry from getting out of hand.

@abowlfulloflemons

see when supplies are getting low and need to be replaced.

Use matching, box-shaped containers all in one color, or use baskets to add a woven texture. Paint your pantry walls or add pretty shelf paper to dress up your space. I've found the more I like a space, the more I want to keep it organized. So if your pantry is pleasing to look at, you'll be more motivated to keep it neat and clean, and it will feel more like a part of your home.

Style ON A BUDGET

Baskets and bins are crucial to organizing the pantry. Once you've decided what you need, shop around for those that fit your style. Do you want natural baskets or galvanized metal bins to fit your rustic style? Or perhaps simple, monochromatic baskets for a more traditional style? If modern is more your vibe, sleek glass containers might be just the thing. For an eclectic look, use colors and textures that complement the rest of your kitchen area.

WHERE TO SHOP

JARS AND CONTAINERS
- T.J.Maxx
- Walmart
- Wayfair

BASKETS AND BINS
- Amazon
- Dollar Tree
- T.J.Maxx
- Walmart

@exceeding.joy

Displaying like items is a great way to make a big impact.

@houseonwinchester

We love installing old chipped doors to add interest. This glass door was previously the front door of an old farmhouse in our area.

@keely.mann

In the pantry, display the items you use most and hide the ones you don't.

@millhousemanor

With a little work, a dark closet can become a bright farmhouse pantry. We built the shelves—which now hold vintage ironstone bowls, cutting boards, and dishes—and painted everything white.

MAKE YOUR HOUSE A *Home*

ALICIA ARMSTRONG
www.OurVintageNest.com
@ourvintagenest

I am a wife and a mom of two who has always had a love for design, but I've never had a way to express it. When I started on Instagram in 2015, it quickly became a creative outlet for me. Finding community on Instagram also filled a void during a difficult time and brought me in contact with many like-minded Christian women. I like to say that it was during this time that "I found my people!" This community has been a blessing that continues to grow. It has also given me opportunities to meet other design bloggers, work with companies big and small, and earn extra income for my family.

MY WHY

I love to share my passion for decorating and encourage others to create a home they love. Interior design doesn't require spending a lot of money, especially if you begin by shopping your own home first, breathing new life into old pieces, and giving them a whole new purpose.

FAVORITE TIPS

- Style your shelves. Adding textures and foliage is key to creating the perfect vignette. If you're looking for more inspiration, my blog is filled with photos and tips.
- Layer. When I design a space, I love to

layer because it adds depth and dimension. Creating a gallery wall is a perfect example of layering.

Motto for Life
Love one another!

FIVE MUST-HAVES

1 CEREAL CONTAINERS

If your family is like mine and loves cereal, it's worth investing in containers. There are all different kinds available, including glass or plastic, with spouts for easy pouring. I found some hotel-style dispensers on Amazon, and my kids love them. (The grown-ups do too!) Containers keep cereal fresh longer than boxes, and they help your pantry look neat and clean.

2 BASKETS AND CONTAINERS

I have multiple baskets in my pantry: one for snacks, one for baking items, one for chips, and one for pasta. You get the idea. Categorize and condense your items into one basket per category. I also have glass containers for flour and sugar. Mine are large jars from Walmart, and they're much prettier than those half-opened bags that spill everywhere.

3 CONTACT PAPER

Pretty contact paper makes a fun statement, but it also allows you to wipe off dirty surfaces. I laid floral contact paper on each shelf in my pantry. The pop of color is inviting and makes the space feel like an extension of the kitchen rather than a neglected space.

4 A LAZY SUSAN

Many pantries have narrow corners with space you either can't see or use. Maximize those spaces with a lazy Susan to hold items you don't use all the time but still want to see and access. Since they can be made from marble to plastic to wood, you can find a lazy Suzan to meet any design style.

5 DOOR ORGANIZERS

There are many types of door organizers. Some hang on doors to create a mini-pantry with multiple shelves. Others are designed to hold brooms, mops, and those other odds and ends you don't want cluttering the floor. I have a wall-mounted organizer that keeps my broom, mop, and duster off the floor and out of sight.

Saving Graces

To each one of us grace has been given.

—EPHESIANS 4:7 NIV

In creating my home, I've learned I need to give myself and my family grace. I especially needed grace when my then-two-year-old son decided to use a permanent marker on the white shiplap of my master bathroom. I needed to give grace because, for him, it was a work of art. He ran to grab my hand and pulled me toward the bathroom to show me what he'd done. He was so proud of his accomplishment and truly wanted me to revel in it with him. To my dismay, I discovered that his artwork was all down the side of the white clawfoot tub, scribbled on the windowsills, and across the white shiplap walls.

My first reaction was complete shock, but his innocent face looking for my approval changed my reaction completely. Yes, we had a conversation about the benefits of using paper instead of walls, and he hasn't repeated that particular bit of artistry, but in that moment I needed to give grace.

After a deep breath and a healthy dose of forgiveness, I moved on. I also learned nail polish remover and lemon essential oil work wonders for removing permanent marker. (If you have your own artist on the loose,

We need grace as we try to create the happy home we've always dreamed of.

check the internet for how-to tips and always test in a more hidden spot first.)

There won't be a time when my home is perfectly clean (except the five minutes after the once-a-month deep cleaning is finished). And there probably won't be a time when I feel it's perfectly decorated or I don't compare myself to a million beautiful homes and second-guess my design decisions. We need grace as we try to create the happy home we've always dreamed of. We need to pat ourselves on the back for trying to build intentional, purpose-filled homes that serve our families. That desire is a beautiful starting point for creating and enjoying your space.

There are many times I fall short—when I've had a long day, the laundry is piled up to my ears, and the dishes are stacked high in the sink. These are days we need to give grace, and sometimes we just need to give ourselves permission to go to bed and try again tomorrow. Regardless of how picture-perfect our homes are (or aren't), there will

always be spaces that need a little (or a lot of) grace: drop zones full of coats and shoes, bills stacked high in the office, ingredients from last Christmas shoved in the back of the pantry. And don't forget the obnoxious toys too big to be hidden. Don't despair! There are solutions and ways to decorate around these problem areas.

On the following pages, you'll find some of my favorite ideas and best advice. But above all, I want you to find grace: grace for yourself, grace for your loved ones, and—yes—grace for all the spaces of your life.

Come with me, and let's explore the beauty found in these saving graces.

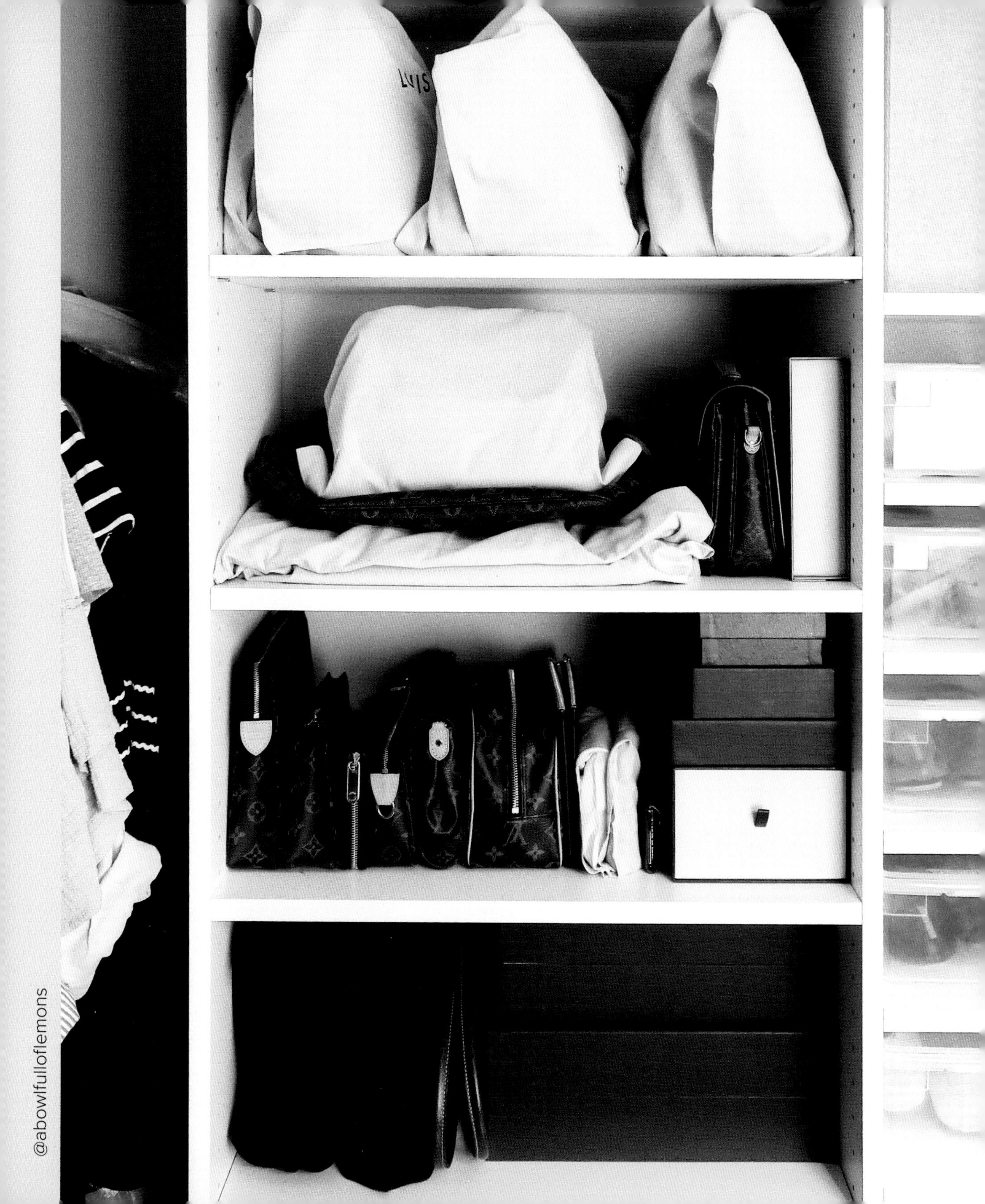

@abowlfulloflemons

Chapter 13

TOP TEN ORGANIZING TIPS

A place for everything and everything in its place.

I've mentioned many ways to stay organized in this book, but this top ten list makes the biggest difference in my everyday upkeep. Although I've mentioned some of these ideas, here is a quick, go-to reference for all your places and spaces that need a little grace.

@abowlfulloflemons

1 Designated drawers for designated items.

It seems so logical, but I know people who don't have a sock drawer or a utensil drawer. How do they know where to put their socks or their forks? Assign one drawer at a time and find a home for the items you see sitting around.

2 A shoe station.

We have a basket in the mudroom where our everyday shoes stay. I've seen people use big barrels, baskets, or shoe racks in the garage.

For my family, taking them upstairs or to a bedroom closet just doesn't work—they need a spot near the door. Have a place to put those shoes where they come off.

3 A mail station.

I have a small bin on my desk where all the bills and papers go, and about once a week I go through them. Having this drop-off spot gives me a place to put that paper clutter until I'm ready to deal with it—and keeps it from spreading through the rest of the house.

4 A zone for keys, change, and charging.

How many times have you lost your keys? For many women, they disappear into the purse (also known as the abyss!), but oftentimes my husband leaves his keys on the counter, where they get lost just as easily amid the shuffle. Keep a basket for keys, a jar for loose change, and a charger for phones in a spot close to where you come and go. Ours is on the kitchen counter. We come in, drop the keys in the basket, empty out our change, and plug in our phones. It just makes life simpler.

5 A bin in the closet for outgrown or seasonal items.

I keep a bin in each of my boys' closets. Once the season changes or my boys grow out of clothes, those items go in the bin. I don't think about it—I just throw it in. Then twice a year during consignment season, I go through the bin. Clothes either go to consignment, Goodwill, storage (for seasonal items that can be worn again), or trash (I have boys, remember?). This system will keep you from constantly going through their clothes. Just toss the discards in the bin until sorting time. And by the way, this works great for teen and grown-up closets too!

6 Toy storage.

Find ways to keep toys out of sight. This is almost impossible with riding toys, scooters, play kitchens, and other big toys, but I always hide my kids' toys as best as I can, and neither of them (maybe by fluke?) makes much of a mess. They take out what they're playing with and put it back when they're done. Baskets and totes are great options for toy storage. Use clear bins for storing LEGOs, superheroes, and other small toys so they're easy to find and kept together.

7 Cleaning products under each sink in the house.

This has helped me so much! When I see a countertop that needs to be cleaned, instead of putting it off because I don't want to search for supplies, I can simply reach under the sink and grab what I need. I also keep a toilet brush behind each toilet. To make it even simpler, I use one cleaner—a Seventh Generation all-purpose cleaner—throughout the house.

8 A cleaned-out fridge and pantry.

Oh, how I hate this job. But I've found it's much more manageable if I clean and purge each time I put in new groceries. So go ahead

and toss a few items here and there as you're loading in the new ones. It helps immensely!

9 A basket for each child.

Each of my boys has a basket that holds what he's currently working on or reading. If it's a puzzle, a book, or a current school project, this is where it goes. If your child has a favorite book or coloring book, put that in there too so each child has his or her portable "office" to carry to the table or playroom. This works just as well for the homework, permission slips, and projects of older kids and teens.

10 A constantly running washing machine and dishwasher.

Dirty clothes and dishes are just reality. To keep the clothes piles under control, my washing machine is almost always running. Now, I have yet to perfect *putting away* the laundry, but I've found it works better if I put things away immediately after folding. I also load and run the dishwasher every night. If the dishwasher is running, it means my kitchen is clean for the night. And my husband and I both agree that waking up to a clean kitchen in the morning helps the day start better. Some people feel this way about making their beds. It just gives you a sense of accomplishment and readiness.

BONUS: Make daily lists. We all have things we do daily: feed the cats, feed the dogs, check the email, do the dishes. So why not make a list and have it ready for you to review each morning? (There are even apps out there to help you with this.) My daily list enables me to say, "Okay, I've done these tasks. Now what is my goal today?" And, yes, I literally talk to myself. (You know you do it too!) That goal can be as simple as getting that laundry put away or as challenging as painting a wall, but I always try to give myself one goal. Be wary of overloading yourself with too many goals—having *one* goal and completing it makes a huge difference. Also, the victory of accomplishing that goal will help you see you've been productive—especially on those days you feel you've been anything but.

Chapter 14

FINDING THE BEST DEALS

A penny saved is a penny earned.

I pride myself on finding the best deals. My husband and I are both frugal and emphasize saving over spending. So I get excited when I find a good deal, and I hate to see people spending a lot of money on décor and other items they can get cheaper elsewhere. So here are my best money-saving tips.

1 Know your sale days.

This applies to many stores. Hobby Lobby, for example, usually rotates their sales every two to three weeks. This means one week their room décor will be on sale, and the next week mirrors, clocks, and knobs will be on sale. They even have an app that shares the weekly ad and offers a 40-percent-off coupon to use on one regularly priced item.

Online stores, such as World Market and Wayfair, also go through a cycle of sales. World Market usually has a twice-a-year friends-and-family sale that features 30 percent off regular prices. Wayfair's biggest sale days usually fall around holidays, but they almost always have a selection of 70-percent-off items. If you have a favorite shop or online store, pay attention to their sale cycles. It can save you a bundle!

2 Shop thrift stores.

Believe it or not, Goodwill has so many treasures that you are doing yourself an injustice if you don't at least glance inside. I outfitted my she shed with baskets for under $3 each, and I've found so many useful dishes and serving pieces there over the years. Ironstone, transferware, silver platters, chairs, baskets, and art—you name it, I've found it at Goodwill. And on one Saturday a month, everything is half off. They even offer coupons online.

Scour multiple Goodwills and other thrift stores. Each one has something different. Ask about their restocking day. Most stores usually have one a day a week when they put out new stock. Go that day. And don't be afraid to dig!

The Habitat for Humanity ReStore is one of my other favorites. You can find some amazing deals on a variety of things, from lamps to furniture to paint supplies.

3 Use social media and shopping apps.

Facebook Marketplace is one of the few reasons I get on Facebook. It's a great way to find antiques, appliances, and décor items. Type in the item you're searching for and *voilà!*—an endless garage sale of items. You can even turn on notifications to alert you when a new item in your category pops up. If you find something you like, ask if the item is still available. And don't be afraid to negotiate. Ask what the lowest amount is they'd

be willing to take. One word of warning: Marketplace can be addicting, so make sure you're buying items you need!

Similarly, the OfferUp app is like the Instagram of deals. All you see are photos. Scroll your heart out to find the item you're looking for, or if you're like me, just browse for the fun of it. You also can turn on notifications to alert you when similar items are restocked. Try using key search words that others might not. For example, search *old desk* instead of simply *desk*. Use *broken* to help you find vintage items to repurpose. And be sure to bargain for the best price.

4 Shop bargain stores.

Visiting discount stores like T.J.Maxx, Marshalls, and Ross can yield decorating treasures. If you're in the South or Midwest, you might live near a store called Bargain Hunt that gets Target's hand-me-downs. I've scored many Hearth & Hand items for half the usual price. Do some research to find similar stores in your area.

5 Compare prices and shop online.

Amazon is one of my go-to stores. I have found fabulous items in every category— kitchen knobs, lighting, beds, mattresses, box springs, home décor, baskets, clothing, dressers, and much more. Amazon also allows you to create a wish list. Add items to it, and Amazon will alert you if the items go up or down in price.

But Amazon isn't the only place for online shopping. Many people are surprised to discover that T.J.Maxx has online shopping as well. And don't forget about Wayfair and Overstock.com. Check multiple sites and compare prices.

this is us

OUR LIFE
OUR STORY
OUR HOME

MAINSTREAM CO.

NO.46 SIXTH STREET, ABOVE MISSION.

COFFEE! COFFEE!

EVERYWHERE BUT NONE TO COMPARE WITH OUR

NORTH STAR BLEND

AT 25 CENTS.

Chapter 15

DECORATING MUSTS

*The most beautiful home is the
one decorated with love.*

Even the best decorators can feel overwhelmed or unsure of where to start. So if you're feeling this way, let me reassure you: making a home is a process, and it doesn't happen overnight. In fact, if you're anything like me, your home and style are constantly evolving. To help you in your journey of making yourself a home, here are the five things I want you to take away from this book.

@simplysoutherncottage

2 Get inspired.

Look through magazines, books, local shop displays, and decorating blogs. Place sticky notes on the pages that inspire you. Later, go back to all your tabbed pages or Pinterest boards and look for recurring design styles or trends. It might surprise you to find you already have a sense of style by what you've picked out. Take note of textures, colors, and design, and consider ways to incorporate those into your own home.

3 Start small.

Reorganize one room at a time or work on one refresh at a time. Do your living room one month, then work your way into the half bath. Take it slow and work within your budget and abilities.

4 When in doubt, decorate the door, the mantel, and the tables.

If your door is decorated with a pretty wreath and welcome mat, you've set the tone for what will be found inside. Take time to clean up your front door and entryway. Commit to changing out your wreath a few times a year and setting out flowers.

Then decorate your mantel. Use greenery, candlesticks, signs, art, or whatever makes you smile. If you don't have a mantel, create and decorate a focal point in your living and

1 Know your *why*.

Determine the purpose for your home and each space in it. Get to know your house.

- What do you want out of the spaces you use?
- What does your family enjoy doing in your home?
- What works where?
- What rooms are used the most?
- Do you want to create a particular atmosphere?

Before you do any decorating, take some time to ponder the purpose of your home.

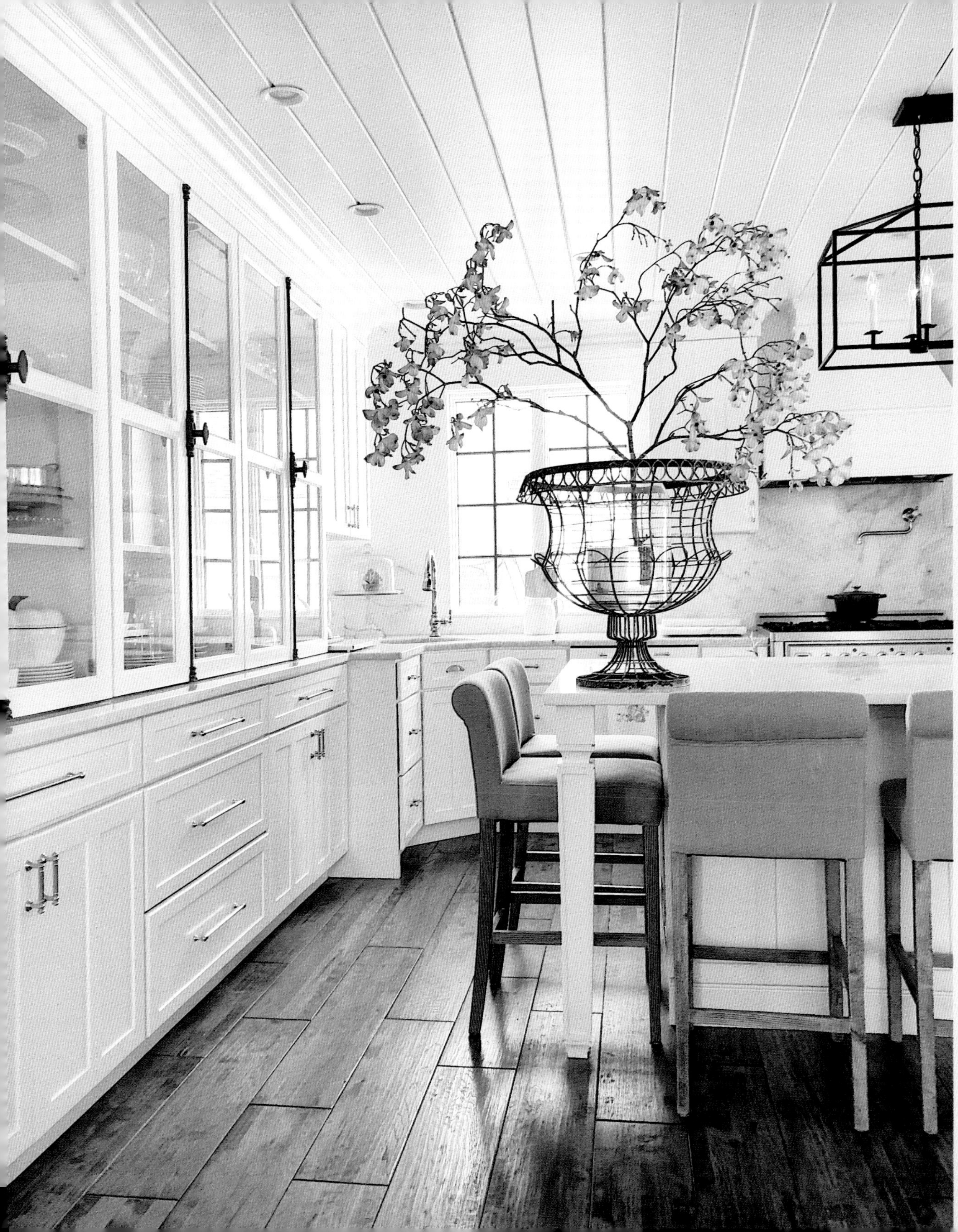

@featherglass

an entertainment center. If all you can muster is the time to decorate a focal point, then do that—and it will go a long way toward giving your room that pulled-together look.

Finally, add some décor to your tables. If you have a coffee table, set out a tray with a few magazines. If you have side tables, add lamps, small picture frames, or coasters. For the dining table, a runner and a floral centerpiece add instant color and style.

5 Give yourself grace.

Grace to know your strengths and grace to know your weaknesses. Creating a home and knowing your style takes time. I have watched my own style evolve over the years, so I now feel confident in knowing what I like and don't like. And tastes can change as we age. That's okay. The joy isn't found only in being done with decorating; it's in the process of making yourself a home.

gathering areas. Perhaps it's a faux fireplace mantel, a gallery wall above your couch, or

My Hope for You

It's my hope that this book will challenge you to start thinking about your home in a different way. To ask yourself not only about your style and favorite colors but about your *why*. What purpose do you want your home and each area in it to serve? Take some time to get to know your home and your family's needs in it. Work with what you have first. From there, you can begin the design process.

I also hope you aren't overwhelmed but rather are encouraged by all the photos, design tools, and tips and tricks I've shared from my own life, along with those from many other smart and talented women (who might be new-to-you friends to follow!).

More than that, I want you to be inspired to dig deep and discover the creativity you have within yourself. You can do this! You can create a home that brings you joy and feels like home. Each page and each story shared is from a woman, maybe just like you, with a vision for her home, herself, and her family. It is my hope that these women and I will inspire you to follow your own journey. Above all, I want you to know this simple truth: she made herself a home, and so can *you*.

Acknowledgments

To God, first and foremost. My relationship with You has always been intimate since I was old enough to speak Your name. I treasure it to the depths of my soul and am so thankful for Your friendship, guidance, companionship, and dedication to my life. With You all things are possible.

To my family, who always believed I was created to share my life through writing. To your endless support, hugs, I-love-yous, and encouragement. You are my world.

To my husband. Your joy for life has perfectly balanced out my soul since I was fourteen. I appreciate your support in all I do. Your willingness to complete anything I ask and the way you dote on me still has me smiling. I will love you until my last breath.

To my boys and future adoptive daughter. You complete me. You have given me purpose, and I will honor, stand by, protect, fight for, and love you till the end.

To my HarperCollins Christian Publishing family. Thank you for taking a chance on a newbie and for believing in my skills enough to pursue this book. Thank you for putting up with my questions and frustrations. It is truly my goal to make you all proud.

To Debbie Nichols, who planted a seed for me at HarperCollins and took the time to share my love and passion so that it might be shared with the world. This generous act of kindness will never be forgotten.

To the many amazing contributors throughout the book. This vision was only possible with your support and willingness to be included. It was truly my greatest pleasure to take you along my journey and share in the beauty of design. I will cherish each and every one of you throughout my journey, and I promise to help support you on yours. You made this book possible, and I will never forget that.

To Grace, my sweet Anne on the hill. Thank you for so patiently and willingly taking photos of my home for this book. You have been and always will be the one I want to capture my family's life through a lens.

To Leslee and her team for our cover photo and other images. Your God-given skill is evident, and we loved working with you. Seeing your passion for photography was beautiful to witness.

To my Instagram and blogging community. I never dreamed I'd have deep friendships virtually. I am here to say that it's possible! What wouldn't be possible is this book without the support, likes, comments, and joy you each have brought me. I do not take my corner of the internet lightly, and you each make me want to get up and create again and again. Thank you!

To my readers. Whether you have never heard of this girl on the cover or you've been supporting me for twenty years, I appreciate you so much. By your purchase and support, I am living my childhood dream. Never did I think at age five, sitting at my grandmother's typewriter, I would have this book to share with the world. I truly hope this book gives your home purpose and helps you create spaces that perfectly fit you and family.

Credits

QUOTE CREDITS

xiii Sally Clarkson and Sarah Clarkson, *The Lifegiving Home: Creating a Place of Belonging and Becoming* (Carol Stream, Illinois: Tyndale Momentum, 2016), 8.

105 John Muir, *Our National Parks* (Boston: Houghton Mifflin, 1901), 56.

113 Ralph Waldo Emerson, *The Complete Works* (New York and Boston: Houghton Mifflin, 1904), https://www.bartleby.com/90/0707.html.

117 Jane Austen, *Emma* (London: John Murray, 1815), 244.

PHOTO CREDITS

PHOTOGRAPHY
Leslee Mitchell

MAKEUP & HAIR
Christin Cook Zito

PHOTOS BY LESLEE MITCHELL PHOTOGRAPHY
vi, 4, 23, 25, 32, 36, 48, 52, 60, 92, 120, 123, 139, 144, 146, 147, 152, 174, 177, 182, 190, 202

PHOTOS BY GRACE ROWE, CLEARLY PHOTOGRAPHY
iii, viii, ix, xviii, xxii, 11, 14, 16, 17, 24, 34, 40, 41, 46, 54, 67, 71, 85, 86, 106, 107, 108, 116, 118, 135, 136, 167, 173, 186, 187, 194

x *winter porch* © Kierste Wade/@oldsaltfarm

xii *book display* © Sara McDaniel/@simplysoutherncottage

xiii *ottoman* © Ellen Sharpe/@featherglass

xiv *pink-and-white bed* © Erin Kern/@cottonstem

xvii *shelves* © Rachael Pancic

xx *casual dining table* © Keely Mann/@keely.mann

formal dining table © Ashley Harrison/@ourvictorianitaliante

xxi *rustic living room* Jenny Zacharewicz/@bigfamilylittlefarmhouse

eclectic living room © Holli Rodrigues/@beesnburlap

3 *dining table* © Angela Rose/@angelarose_diyhome

coffee table © Spacecrafting Photography

7 *entryway drop zone* © Megan Schmidt/@theschmidthome

8 *front doors* © Rachel Van Kluyve/@crateandcottage

9 *pink flowers* © Ellen Sharpe/@featherglass

12 *5* © Holli Rodrigues/@beesnburlap

101 *z headboard* © Valerie Paulus Photography
black lamp © Valerie Paulus Photography
fireplace © Valerie Paulus Photography

103 *bunk beds* © Katie Sullivan/@prettydomesticated

104 *white Adirondack chairs* © Ellen Sharpe/@featherglass

109 *brown Adirondack chairs* © Keely Mann/@keely.mann

110 *white porch swing* © Sara McDaniel/@simplysoutherncottage
brown porch swing © Brooke Jones/@plankandpillow

111 *pool* © Brooke Jones/@plankandpillow
pumpkins © Karen Snyder/@sanctuaryhomedecor

112 *portrait* © Leslie Saeta/@my100yearoldhome

113 *brick fireplace* © Leslie Saeta/@my100yearoldhome
three stools © Leslie Saeta/@my100yearoldhome
metal vases © Leslie Saeta/@my100yearoldhome

114 *porch dining table* © Karen Snyder/@sanctuaryhomedecor
screen room © Tracey Jazmin/@tracey.jazmin

115 *white bench* © Spacecrafting Photography

119 *white mudroom* © Tracey Jazmin/@tracey.jazmin

124 *library* © Carrie Johnson/@lovecarriej

126 *blue wall* © Brooke Jones/@plankandpillow
black desk © Katie Sullivan/@prettydomesticated

127 *white curtains* © Katrina Morris/@themorrismanor
white desk © Sara McDaniel/@simplysoutherncottage

128 *portrait* © BKN Creative

129 *white desk* © BKN Creative

131 *blue rug* © BKN Creative
white cabinet © Theresa Halverson/@millhousemanor

132 *green wall* © Jackie Hempel/@finding_lovely

137 *pink flower* © Carrie Johnson/@lovecarriej

140 *checkered bedspread* © Carrie Johnson/@lovecarriej
playroom © Jessica Wasserman/@jesswasserman

141 *teepee* © Kierste Wade/@oldsaltfarm
metal chairs © Ashley Harrison/@ourvictorianitaliante

142 *portrait* © Erin Kern/@cottonstem

143 *bunk beds* © Erin Kern/@cottonstem
bench © Erin Kern/@cottonstem
playroom © Erin Kern/@cottonstem

145 *pink bags* © Erin Kern/@cottonstem

148 *laundry sign* © Kierste Wade/@oldsaltfarm

154 *portrait* © Allison Aars/@thefestivefarmhouse

155 *wood bench* © Allison Aars/@thefestivefarmhouse
white stove © Allison Aars/@thefestivefarmhouse
checkered bedspread © Allison Aars/@thefestivefarmhouse

156 *ladder* © Brittany Hislop/@white.farmhouse
white lockers © Stacey Rossetti/@farmhousechic4sure

157 *bucket light fixtures* © Jenny Zacharewicz/@bigfamilylittlefarmhouse
black rain boots © Brooke Jones/@plankandpillow

158 *portrait* © Toni Hammersley/@abowlfulloflemons

159 *hangers* © Toni Hammersley/@abowlfulloflemons
kitchen shelves © Toni Hammersley/@abowlfulloflemons
closet shelves © Toni Hammersley/@abowlfulloflemons

161 *sunflowers* © Sara McDaniel/@simplysoutherncottage

162 *green door* © Jenny Zacharewicz/@bigfamilylittlefarmhouse

165 *glass cabinet* © Toni Hammersley/@abowlfulloflemons

168 *blue jars* © Shelby Hauenstein @exceeding.joy
green apples © Danelle Harvey/@houseonwinchester

169 *clear baskets* © Keely Mann/@keely.mann
brown closet doors © Theresa Halverson/@millhousemanor

170 *portrait* © Alicia J. Armstrong/@ourvintagenest

171 *EAT sign* © Alicia J. Armstrong/@ourvintagenest
green pillows © Alicia J. Armstrong/@ourvintagenest
white bench © Alicia J. Armstrong/@ourvintagenest

178 *bags* © Toni Hammersley/@abowlfulloflemons

180 *cleaning supplies* © Toni Hammersley/@abowlfulloflemons

184 *stools* © Karen Snyder/@sanctuaryhomedecor

189 *books in fireplace* © Laura Opfel/@threesonsfarmhouse

192 *fireplace* © Sara McDaniel/@simplysoutherncottage

193 *white cabinets* © Ellen Sharpe/@featherglass

About the Author

Rachel Van Kluyve is a Nashville stay-at-home mom turned momtrepreneur. Most days you can find her in a messy bun and yoga pants wrangling two boys while running a real estate business, homeschooling, DIYing, and keeping up with her décor passions. Rachel loves a good challenge and to be moving constantly, but she also loves to pause for family dance parties in the kitchen. She's known for her thrifty finds and the ability to make every dollar count. Amazon is her go-to, and she loves to say she has elegant taste on a Target budget. She is most passionate about her faith, her husband (and high school sweetheart), her two boys, her writing, and serving silently behind the scenes.

Although Rachel has a degree in journalism and English, her passion for writing springs from generations of poets before her, and since childhood, she's had an innate love for writing stories and keeping a journal. Her penchant for design stems from going to antique malls and flea markets with her mother, who was constantly changing and redecorating their home, while her deep love of all things old was sparked by her historian father. Although decorating on a budget is her passion, repurposing old things is even better—perhaps because every piece has a story.

The summer of 2017 was the move-in date for her self-designed farmhouse on twenty acres outside of Nashville. It's from here she shares her farmhouse journey, her décor, and her deep convictions of creating an intentional home on her blog and social media. It's her desire to encourage others to see their own talents and gifts and to be confident in who they were created to be.

You can find Rachel at www.CrateandCottage.com and @crateandcottage.